GREAT LAKES
DISASTERS

WAYNE LOUIS KADAR

D0778331

Avery Color Studios, Inc.
Gwinn, Michigan

© 2011 Avery Color Studios, Inc.

ISBN: 978-1-892384-62-1

Library of Congress Control Number: 2011904324

First Edition 2011

10   9   8   7   6   5   4   3   2

Published by Avery Color Studios, Inc.
Gwinn, Michigan 49841

TABLE OF CONTENTS

I dedicate this book to my wife Karen, our children, Brandon, Kasie and Grant and our grandchildren.

"Those who cannot remember the past are condemned to repeat it."

George Santayana

INTRODUCTION

The states surrounding the Great Lakes: Michigan, Wisconsin, Illinois, Minnesota, Indiana, Ohio, Pennsylvania, New York, and the Canadian Province of Ontario have fallen victim to many disasters. Some are classified as natural disasters, storms, tornadoes and floods, yet many disasters that have befallen the Great Lakes Region are the consequence of man.

As man populated the region, the disasters followed. The primary means of transportation in the region was on rivers and the lakes and in the early history of man in the Great Lakes region most disasters were related to the water.

More people migrated to the area and began clearing forests for farming and fires resulted. Some fires were out of control and the result was disastrous. People moved to cities and suffered the consequences

associated with larger populations. Yet other disasters that occurred in the region were the result of man's own hand in the pursuit of riches. Mining hundreds of feet below the surface can have a disastrous outcome.

Innovation and progress can be the blame for some disasters. Trains, automobiles and airplanes are all great conveniences but also can be responsible for large-scale death and destruction.

The disasters in this book are just a few of the catastrophes that have befallen the Great Lakes Region. Some are the result of man's own incompetence while in other disasters man was the victim.

Mark Twain did not have much faith in mankind when he penned;

"It is not worthwhile to try to keep history from repeating itself, for man's character will always make the preventing of the repetitions impossible."

Yet the importance of studying the disasters of our past cannot be so understated. We must study the catastrophes so we can learn from them and prevent them from occurring again.

THE GREAT FIRES OF 1871

The Great Peshtigo Fire

Entire villages and towns were destroyed; hotels, general merchandise stores, the apothecary, livery stables and the animals tied inside, saloons, mills, churches, and homes all burned to ashes as a raging fire swept across northern Wisconsin, parts of Michigan's Upper and Lower Peninsulas and Northern Illinois. Crops in the field, and those laid up as winter storage were devoured and thousands of Midwest residents lost their lives.

The summer of 1871 was hot and dry. Crops withered in the fields from a lack of rain. Creeks dried up. Swamps, normally always wet, dried up until the moist soil dried and cracked. Decades of accumulated leaves fallen from hardwood trees and the thick layer of pine needles were not able to insulate the ground moisture, rather they turned to tinder ready to ignite.

The small northern Wisconsin towns and villages in 1871 were experiencing dramatic population growth as immigrants from Europe migrated to the area to fell trees in the vast virgin forests. Along the rivers and creeks, scores of sawmills were being built by speculators trying to cash in on the lumber boom.

The village of Peshtigo, a rural community in northern Wisconsin, was ideally situated on the banks of the Peshtigo River. The river provided a means of transportation for freight down river to the waters of Green Bay and Lake Michigan and also for floating logs from the forest to the sawmills in Peshtigo.

The American Midwest was experiencing the largest growth in population in its short history. The United States open immigration policies invited immigrants from Europe to move to the United States promising them a better life. They sailed across the Atlantic to ports such as New York and Boston. Many traveled to Buffalo, New York by train or barge on the Erie Canal then took a lake boat to various cities on the Great Lakes.

The immigrants came to the Midwest to clear and farm the land, log the vast virgin forests. Chicago, Detroit, Toledo, Cleveland and others

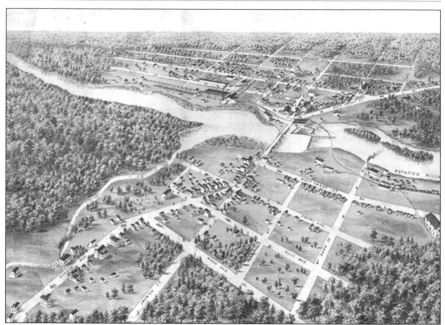

An 1871 map of Peshtigo, Wisconsin. From the United States Library of Congress.

were growing at a rapid rate and there was huge demand for wood to build their cities.

The standard accepted method of logging in 1871 was to send lumberjacks to the woods and cut everything standing; clear-cutting. The lumberjacks cut the limbs and small branches off the trunk and a team of horses or oxen dragged the tree trunks to the river. The limbs and branches, called slash, were left laying in the clearing.

The slash laying in the fields dried and often caught fire. It wasn't unusual to see fires in the fields or for there to be a constant haze of smoke. Small fires were a constant in northern Wisconsin in the 1870s. Farm families and town residents were accustomed to the smell and haze of smoke and seeing the orange glow of a fire on the horizon at night.

The ships sailing on the Great Lakes also experienced the fires in the forests. There are many reports of ships sailing on Lake Michigan sometimes becoming lost in smoke and collisions when visibility was reduced due to the smoke blowing offshore.

The fires were the result of many reasons; farmers burned the piles of slash and the stumps in the newly cleared fields in preparation for

THE GREAT FIRES OF 1871

cultivation of the land. Or as the railroads were being built, Northern Wisconsin trees and brush that was cut away for the track bed was left laying along the right of way. Embers escaping from the coal fired steam locomotives often ignited the brush piles.

Hunters in the woods were often not as cautious with their campfires as they should have been. Sometimes the campfire got out of control, or the fire was left smoldering and resulted in igniting a nearby field or woodlot.

Some fires were caused by natural causes. Lightning strikes were and still are responsible for many fires but lightning was not the cause of the fires in the summer of 1871, there weren't any storms.

On October 8, 1871 all of the contributing factors united with cataclysmic results.

The numerous small fires caused by any number of reasons burned uncontrolled. The drought had robbed the fields and forests of moisture leaving dried and highly combustible trees and brush to feed the fire's insatiable hunger. The small fires burned together forming larger fires until they formed one solitary huge fire.

The families living in the outlying areas of Peshtigo, Wisconsin watched the glowing orange sky at night and were concerned, but it was a sight that was common since there was always a fire burning. Yet, on the nights of the first week of October 1871, the glow was more brilliant, the evening breeze a bit warmer, the persistent odor and haze from smoke more intense, and the occasional glowing ember blowing aloft on the wind more frequent.

The destructive power of a forest fire. From Wikipedia Commons.

The families were concerned but not terrified. Fires started and the rains came and extinguished them. But, this year was different because no rain fell. Rather, the oppressive heat of the unusually hot and dry summer gave way to a dry and warm fall and the fires continued to burn.

The blaze grew unabated, feeding off the withered and dead crops in the fields, the dried up swamps revealing the very combustible peat soil, the slash from logging left in the clearings and the forests with their parched leaves.

Another factor, which turned the smaller fires into the massive monster of destructive power, was a weather pattern that swept across the area. Strong winds blowing from the south fanned the flames and carried burning embers from the fires. The embers landed on new sources of fuel; trees, barns, houses and ignited them almost instantly. An eyewitness account described it as if the sky was raining fire.

People living in the country hoped the fires would miss their homes but planned for the worse. A rope was strung from the house to the barn as they did in winter blizzards. The farmer could hold the rope to guide him to and from the barn in periods of reduced visibility whether a blinding snowstorm or blinding smoke. The women and children were instructed to seek shelter in the root cellar if the flames came, or to lower themselves into the well to be shielded from the fire's heat.

The families first heard a roar in the distance, saw the eerie orange glow in the sky and choked on the thick, blinding smoke. The creatures of the forest, deer, birds, bear, raccoon, and fox which normally avoided human contact, ran through the farmyards, racing from the approaching fire.

The red-hot embers blown on the wind landed on the fields and buildings. The people ran from their burning homes to root cellars. Many children, the aged and infirm collapsed from the acrid smoke filling their lungs and robbing them of the oxygen their bodies so desperately needed. They fell choking, vomiting and dying of asphyxiation.

The immense fire, fueled by the drought and blown by the winds, devoured anything in its path; homes, barns, crops, forests were all consumed by the fire's destructive power.

Several sought shelter in shallow creeks or ponds, not dried up by the drought. Some died a horrible death as the intense heat of the fire boiled the water.

Burning embers falling from the sky ignited the hair, bonnets, and clothing of frightened people. They ran from the fire looking for safety until the blaze over took them and they fell in the horrific pain of their burning flesh, resulting in unconsciousness and death.

THE GREAT FIRES OF 1871

Some lucky people avoided the falling embers and the lung clogging smoke but were killed by the intense heat of the advancing fire. The superheated wind blew from the fire, instantly igniting anything in its path: hair, clothing, flesh. The poor people never had a chance.

For the few who reached their root cellars, many did not find the salvation they expected.

As the roar of the fire passed overhead, the people sheltering below in the root cellars felt the heat of the passing flames but the fire consumed the oxygen and they died of affixiation, or for others the passing fire sucked the air out of their lungs. When they took their next breath they inhaled superheated air causing a painful but quick death.

After the fire passed, individuals and sometimes entire families were found harboring in the farm well. The intense heat and the choking smoke had overcome some while others drown in their own well.

The residents of Peshtigo watched the glowing orange sky creep closer to town. They knew that the homes and farms of some of their friends were destroyed. They felt for them but now the fire was marching east threatening to destroy their lives.

The Peshtigo fire department with 1871 equipment, a horse drawn pump manually operated, stood ready to make a stand against the advancing conflagration.

When the fire arrived, the few volunteers fought the heat, the blowing embers and the thick acrid smoke until their hoses and pump caught on fire. They had no recourse but to run for the river with the rest of town.

The fire roared into town blown on the near hurricane force winds generated by the weather system affecting the area, combined with the superheated whirlwinds created by the intensity of the blaze.

The fire blew in unabated, consuming everything in its path. The hotels, the livery with horses tied in their stalls, the Peshtigo town hall with all of the area birth, death and population records were quickly reduced to ashes; nothing was spared.

The inhabitants of Peshtigo ran to the river hoping it would offer them salvation. Many perished as they were overcome by the smoke and fell choking and gagging, some burned as their clothing ignited from the hail of flaming debris dropping from the sky, others died as the superheated air blowing robbed the breath from their lungs. Many others were trampled by horses and cows in a frenzied stampede. Families were separated, children ran screaming for mothers and mothers cried out for their missing children.

The Peshtigo Fire Department fire apparatus was similar to this late 1800 equipment.

Some residents were pushed down and run over by their friends and neighbors. They were killed or laid on the side of the road too injured to save themselves, waiting for the fire to take their lives.

Those who reached the banks of the river were not guaranteed salvation. Many who made it to the river waded into the cooling waters only to be pushed aside by others seeking safety. They were shoved under the surface and drown at the feet of their friends. Several were killed when the wood bridge connecting the two halves of the city ignited and collapsed casting the people on the bridge into the river and others died when burning debris floating downstream struck them.

It was thought the fire would stop when it reached the banks of the river, it would simply run out of fuel. But the fire, blown by the cyclonic winds, leaped over the river and took aim on that side of town.

Some residents ran the seven miles towards the cool waters of Green Bay hoping to be saved. Many never made it to the bay.

Some children, older and/or infirm adults or others overcome by exhaustion fell to the ground in their attempt to get to Green Bay, only to be crushed below the wheels of the horse or oxen drawn wagons racing along the road.

THE GREAT FIRES OF 1871

The Peshtigo Fire Memorial in Peshtigo, Wisconsin.

For those who reached the waters of Green Bay, many met the same fate as their friends had in the Peshtigo River.

The forest fire burned up to the edge of Green Bay; in some areas the hot burning embers were carried on the wind to the offshore islands of the Door Peninsula. The wooded islands were soon denuded of all vegetation by the raging inferno.

The Great Peshtigo Fire, as it would be known, had raced across Northern Wisconsin burning over 1,500,000 acres. When the rains finally came and suppressed the flames, the devastation wrought on the area was unbelievable. The fire burned the counties of Oconto, Brown, Door, Kewaunee, Marinette, and Michigan's Menominee County in the Upper Peninsula. Twelve towns and villages were destroyed, almost 2,000 square miles of land was burned and tragically, between 1,200 and 2,200 people lost their lives, a great many in Peshtigo where over half the village population perished.

The amount of people killed in the Great Peshtigo Fire has and never will be exactly determined. The population of the village and the outlying areas was growing as people immigrated to the area to work in the woods and to farm the cleared land and what records that were kept regarding population were lost when the village hall burned.

The Peshtigo Fire has the dubious distinction of being the most devastating fire in recorded history of North America.

The Peshtigo blaze led to new forest management programs by the federal government. Less wasteful harvesting techniques were implemented to prevent future large-scale destruction of forests. New fire policies on fighting and prevention developed in the area due to the Peshtigo blaze.

The Michigan Fires

The Peshtigo Fire, which ravaged the Northern Wisconsin countryside and then destroyed the village of Peshtigo was not the only fire to lay siege on the Great Lakes region. On October 8, 1871, the same date of the

Peshtigo fire, the Michigan towns of Manistee, Holland, Port Huron and the "Thumb" of lower Michigan's mitten were visited by a monstrous inferno.

The cause of the fires were the result of the same wasteful logging methods practiced in Wisconsin. Large tracts of forests were clear cut leaving the branches of the trees to dry, rot and become tinder waiting for ignition.

The farming practices of the era, fires intentionally set to clear fields or burn out stumps left from logging, often resulted in out-of-control blazes that spread to other farms, forests or homes, along with hunters who were careless with campfires which sometimes burned into larger fires.

In the Northern Michigan town of Manistee on October 8, 1871, a fire broke out about 9:00 am in a field. The Fire Brigade rushed to the scene and pumped water on the growing fire. The fires threatened to burn that section of town, but through the heroic efforts of the firemen the blaze was put down before much damage was done.

MICHIGAN FIRES.

The Terrible Devastation on the Lake , hore.

Huron City, Sand Beach, Elm Creek, White Rook and Forestville Completely Destroyed.

Partial Destruction of Other Places.

SEVERAL PERSONS BURNED TO DEATH.

Two Thirds of the Population of Huron and Sanilac Counties Homeless.

THE CITY OF MANISTEE ALMOST WHOLLY CONSUMED.

The Fires in the Saginaw Valley Region.

THE FIRES ON THE LAKE SHORE.
Special Dispatch to the Detroit Free Press.
RICHMONDVILLE, October 13, 1871.
The latest intelligence says that Huron City is completely burned, Port Hope partly destroyed, Sand Beach has only two buildings left, and Elm Creek is in the same condition. Rock Falls has escaped thus far. White Rock and Forestville are completely

During the early afternoon, the wind increased in velocity until it was blowing at gale force. The weather system that had fanned the flames in Wisconsin had reached the Michigan coast.

The alarm whistle sounded alerting the citizens of yet another fire; the Magill & Canfield mill was ablaze. The stacks of dry lumber, mountains of sawdust waste and the parched wooden structures of the mill ignited and quickly burned. The fire, in just a short time, destroyed the large main building, the boarding house, the stable, the dock and the shops.

At nightfall an ominous orange glow could be seen to the southwest of town. The majestic pine forest that grew along the Lake Michigan shoreline was burning.

The conflagration raced up the shoreline. Another fire whistle could be heard blaring above the wind's roar, as the fire reached the mouth of the

THE GREAT FIRES OF 1871

Manistee River. The area held several acres of dried out sawdust, piles of lumber waiting to be shipped out and thousands of cords of slab wood used as fuel for the steam tugs. Also in the path of the fire were the sawmill, several tug boats and schooners tied at the pier, and the residences and boarding houses.

Only a few boats were able to sail into the lake for safety. Most other boats and buildings were devoured by the inferno. The government lighthouse was not spared and it too was consumed by the insatiable appetite of the monster.

The next front of the blaze came from the south where the fire was being blown into a firestorm by the high velocity winds. Burning fragments and debris were carried aloft to settle on buildings, dried fields and woodlots. The farms to the south of town were devastated; fields, fences, homes, outbuildings and animals were reduced to ashes.

Men, women and children on horseback, in wagons, and on foot ran from the flames. They wore whatever clothing they could grab in haste, some without shoes, without coats, some in nightshirts.

The wind whipped cinders and burning debris from the farms were blown towards town.

The dead hemlock forest near town had ignited. The fire jumped from dried out tree to another; the dead forest was devoured in just minutes.

Horses pulled the fire department's steam water pump near the flames where they made a valiant stand but in the end the men had to admit defeat and retreat from the unrelenting conflagration to save themselves. The steam pump and fire hoses burned on the street.

There was nothing to stop the advance of the flames, the river was easily crossed by the embers on the tornado strength wind. The fire burned unabated marching through town and the surrounding areas until the winds began to subside in the early morning hours. But the damage had been done

Morning's light revealed the extent of the destruction; the bridge had burned, houses with their family treasures, barns with animals and winter's supply of feed, the inventory of stores, saw mills with their equipment, piles of logs waiting to be sawn into lumber and boards ready to be shipped, schools, churches, and tugboats and schooners unable to escape the blaze were destroyed on that 8th day of October, 1871.

The 1871 fire visited the city of Holland on the southwest side of Michigan. In 1871 the town was only about 25 years in existence, but in the early morning hours of October 9, most of the town was destroyed by a raging inferno that blew on tornado-like winds.

GREAT LAKES DISASTERS

Detroit Free Press.

DETROIT, MICHIGAN, FRIDAY, OCTOBER 13, 1871.

NUMBER 50.

THE LAKE SHORE FIRES.

Miles and Miles of Flames.

EVERY VESTIGE OF CIVILIZATION BEING SWEPT AWAY.

Statements of Some of the Suffering Victims.

A score or more of men, women and children arrived in this city yesterday, by boat and rail, from the up-country counties, and the statements made by them in regard to the woods fires are appalling. All of them have suffered the loss of every dollar of property, and some

The town of Holland was home to 2,400 men women, and children and the town was enjoying growth and prosperity. Great Lakes ships and the railroad delivered and received goods, agricultural products grew well in the soil and were in demand in nearby Chicago, and several manufacturing concerns had been established in the area.

Like the rest of the Midwest, Holland had been experiencing a severe drought. Crops withered in the field and small fires were a usual occurrence.

The wind gradually increased throughout the day on Sunday, October 8, 1871; small fires grew and advanced on the town but the firefighters were able to contain them. But by midnight, the same winds that blew through Wisconsin and carried hot ash and cinders to Peshtigo approached Holland, Michigan.

By 1:00 on the morning of October 9, the winds began to blow and whip the small fires into a raging fury.

The hurricane force winds blew the flames and flaming embers aloft and carried them to the southern end of the town. The Third Reformed Church and the tannery were the first buildings consumed by the beast. The burning wood shingles of the church and the piles of burning bark from the tannery easily ignited and their fragments were carried by the strength of the wind towards town starting other fires wherever they landed.

What man had toiled to create for over twenty-five years, the fire had destroyed in just over two hours. The devastation of Holland was complete, the destruction included 210 homes, 75 stores, shops and offices, 15 manufacturing facilities, 5 churches, 3 hotels, 45 other buildings, 5 docks and warehouses, 1 tugboat and several miscellaneous boats; 250 dead horses, cattle and pigs were later found amid the ruins.

Not a fencepost, a bit of the wooden walk, or any remains of wood foundations were left. And more than 300 families were without shelter and left destitute.

THE GREAT FIRES OF 1871

Yet with the almost total destruction of the town of Holland there was only one fatality. Mrs. J. Toik, a widow of age, was killed in the inferno that consumed Holland, Michigan.

The west side of Michigan was not the only area in the state to feel the hot breath of the fire monster. Port Huron and the communities to its north fell victim to an October 8 fire as well.

The small fire brigade fought a small fire on the outskirts of the vital port city of Port Huron. But as with the other fires, they lost control of the blaze when the winds freshened and grew to a gale and beyond. The fire leaped over the firemen and soon a wall of fire invaded the town.

To the north in the small villages of White Rock, Forester and Forestville the blaze marched unabated across the forests consuming anything in its path: trees, barns, houses, machinery, and people.

From the west to the east coast of Michigan and points between, the fires broke out on October 8, 1871. Holland and Manistee burned on the Lake Michigan side of the state and on Lake Huron, parts of Michigan's Thumb area and a section of Port Huron were destroyed.

A blaze also cut a swath from Lake Michigan to Lake Huron across the state. The area was sparsely populated and few villages and homesteads were destroyed, but thousands of acres of prime Michigan lumber were reduced to ash within hours.

The Chicago Fire

On October 8, 1871, northern Wisconsin and rural Michigan were not the only fires to break out in America's Midwest. The same day of the Peshtigo fire which destroyed almost a million and half acres of farmland and forests, hundreds of buildings and killed thousands, was the same date that several cities, towns, and villages in Michigan were ravaged by fire, killing hundreds and devouring more than a million acres of forest and farmland. But it was also the same date of the Great Chicago Fire.

In the history of America, the 1871, Chicago Fire is more well known than the fires that left Peshtigo and parts of Michigan in ruin. The Chicago fire burned far fewer acres than the other fires and far less people were killed but the large city of Chicago, with a population in the hundreds of thousands, captivated attention throughout the world.

On the evening of October 8, 1871 residents of Chicago were alerted by the clanging of the fire bell. Yet, few took notice, the drought which they had been experiencing of late was responsible for several small fires breaking out around the city and the bell had been sounding frequently in the past few weeks.

An artists depiction of Chicago burning.

Most residents didn't bother counting the strikes of the bell, which indicated the location of the fire. As their rural cousins in Wisconsin and Michigan, they had become complacent; they were accustomed to the smoky haze on the horizon, the smell of smoke and the frequent fire bells.

About 8:30 pm a fire broke out in the alley behind 137 Dekoven Street in the barn of Patrick and Catherine O'Leary. A watchman in the courthouse tower noticed the small fire but he incorrectly determined the location and sent the fire brigade to the wrong address. By the time the firemen arrived at the O'Leary barn it was completely engulfed. The wind blew a shower of burning fragments to adjoining buildings.

By 10:00 pm on October 8 the fire bell clanged without stopping, the general alarm indicated the small fire had grown larger. Now people took notice, they jumped out of bed to look out the window and were greeted with a menacing orange hue in the sky to the southwest.

With the strong southwest wind fanning the flames, the firemen were unable to control the blaze and it quickly spread, consuming whatever was in its path; the docks, sawmill and piles of lumber drying on the banks of the south branch of the Chicago River. Even the oil and waste floating on the river caught on fire.

THE GREAT FIRES OF 1871

The blaze on its relentless march reached the gasworks and it went up with an explosion. The brick courthouse, built to be fireproof, was no match for the fire and it burst into flames as did the wooden State Street bridge.

The poor Irish neighborhood of Conley's Patch was swallowed up in flames. The blaze blown on the wind consumed the neighborhood so fast that many of the residents did not have a opportunity to run. They were overcome by smoke or the heat or were burned to death in their squalid homes.

The Chicago Courthouse seen through the ruins of the First National Bank.

A photograph of the damage caused by the 1871 fire. A New York Times
Photograph.

Sometime after 2:00 am the fire jumped the main branch of the Chicago
River turning the north district of the city into a sea of flames. The
waterworks plant went quickly; no more water was pumped through the cities
water mains thus ending all chances of the firemen to extinguish the blaze.

The lumberyards and Illinois Central Railroad yard was destroyed
along with the McCormick Reaper Works.

People on horseback and riding in wagons stacked high with furniture
and personal items raced along the streets filled with men, women and
children trying to escape Those on foot were pushed aside and trampled.
Hot and flaming cinders rained down on them. Many people had run from
their homes with only the clothes on their back; some ran still dressed in
their sleeping attire.

THE GREAT FIRES OF 1871

For some their clothing showing signs of char where the cinders had ignited them, for some unfortunate souls their clothing became consumed and they ran down the street fully engulfed in flames until they collapsed from the pain of their burning flesh.

Thousands collected on the shore of Lake Michigan. They stood there huddled in a mass hoping the flames would not reach that far but when the wind blown flames licked at them, they waded into the cool water. Wet blankets and overcoats were held over their heads to ward off the shower of embers falling on them.

Thousands more tried to avoid the inferno by heading north. They found salvation at Lincoln Park in the city's northeast section. Still more people continued further north towards the prairie. They rested there hoping they were safe, until the firestorm blew in on the winds and chased them out.

A map of Chicago showing the burned area from the 1871 Great Chicago Fire.

The fire burned for over 24 hours before the winds subsided and a light rain fell slowing the advance of the flames. As survivors surveyed the remains of their city, they found that a 4-mile long by ¾-mile wide section of the city, over 2000 acres, was reduced to not much more than piles of collapsed buildings, ash and charcoal.

More than 17,500 buildings, 73 miles of wooden roads, 120 miles of wood sidewalks and 2000 wood lampposts were destroyed.

An estimated 200 – 300 people were killed and thousands more would live bearing the scars from burns they sustained running from the blaze, and 90,000 people were left homeless.

It was originally printed that Mrs. O'Leary's cow kicked over a lantern, which started the Great Chicago fire, but a reporter twenty-two years after

A drawing that appeared in newspapers around the world showing Mrs. O'Learys cows starting the Great Chicago Fire in 1871.

the fire admitted he had made it up to sensationalize the start of the fire. But Mrs. O'Leary lived in shame and despair the remainder of her life, taunted by neighbors and strangers alike for being responsible for killing so many people and destroying a large part of a major American city.

THE GREAT STORM OF 1913

As sure as there is snow in the winter, fall storms will occur on the Great Lakes. November is well known for its horrendous storms that turn the Great Lakes into a boiling cauldron of wind and waves.

Every fall there are storms of intense velocity but there is one storm that stands far out from the others, the "Great Storm of 1913."

The 1913 storm, often referred to as a "White Hurricane"; a storm on freshwater with winds of hurricane intensity, is widely recognized as the worst storm to ever take aim on the Great Lakes. In terms of the number of dead and missing sailors and the destruction of ships, it was indeed a horrendous natural disaster.

The storm began as a weak low-pressure Arctic front coming down in a southeast direction from Canada. On November 8, 1913, the government Weather Bureau issued a storm warning for the Great Lakes and the red flags with a black center square were raised at all ports along the lakes to tell mariners of the impending storm.

PORT HURON AND THUMB ARE SWEPT

Sixty Mile Gale Causes Great Damage, While Heavy Snowfall Demoralizes Traffic on All Transportation Lines Within the City

Lake Huron Is Whipped Into Fury and Mountainous Waves Leave Trail of Destruction in Their Wake—Night of Terror Is Spent By Many Passengers on Storm-Bound Electric Cars

The warnings did not hold most ships in port. It was towards the end of the season and the captains were under pressure from the shipping companies to make as many trips as possible before winter ice closed the season.

In addition to the Arctic front bearing down on the lakes, there was an intense storm system tracking north. As it neared the Arctic front, the warmer southern storm changed course towards the northwest as it began to absorb the cold air. The southern storm, heavy with moisture, combined with the cold Arctic air over the Great Lakes basin.

Lakes Michigan and Superior fell victim to the intense winds, gigantic waves and snow squalls of the Arctic front. Lake Erie was assaulted by the leading edge of the southern storm but Lake Huron was pounded by the full brunt of the combined storms.

Lakeside communities in Michigan and Ontario were paralyzed with up to two feet of snow and the high winds caused drifts several feet high.

Storms of this magnitude usually last for four or five hours then pass on, but the storm of November 1913 wreaked havoc on the lakes for over three days!

Smaller ships sought shelter during the storm but several large Great Lakes steamships ventured out on lakes even though storm warnings had been issued.

The captains of the large steel ships relied on their knowledge of the lakes and weather. They also had great confidence in their vessels. But they had never sailed into a storm of such catastrophic proportions as the storm that assaulted the lakes on those November days.

Ships that had successfully sailed through the storm later related the horror they endured during the passage. They told of waves crashing down on the length of the ship, the winds that threatened to blow the ship into the trough of the waves, the windows in pilothouses and skylights of engine rooms smashed, lifeboats ripped from their davits and the violent rolling and pitching of the ships in the 30-plus foot seas.

The storm wreaked havoc on the lakes for three days leaving in its wake 19 vessels either cast aground or lost and at least 235 sailors killed. The exact number will never be known.

The following are some of the ships that were out on the lake and assaulted by the storm.

The 436 foot steel freighter *Argus* was only

MANY SHIPS AT MERCY OF WIND AND SEA

Never in Marine History Have Lakes Been Lashed Into Such Fury and Anxiety Is Felt For Many Vessels Which Have Not Yet Reported

THE GREAT STORM OF 1913

The Hydrus. *From the collection of the Port Huron Museum.*

10 years old at the time of her loss. As she steamed on Lake Huron along the Canadian shore, the *Argus* broke in half and sank near Kincardin, Ontario taking her crew of twenty-five with her.

The *Hydrus*, like the *Argus*, was 436 feet in length and also launched in 1903. The *Hydrus* was down-bound along the Michigan shore with a cargo of iron ore in winds nearing 90 miles per hour and waves taller than a three-story building.

The huge steel ship, weighed down by its cargo, probably became trapped in the trough of the waves, its cargo shifted and she rolled over and sank off Lexington, Michigan, with her crew of twenty eight.

The five-year-old, *John A. McGean*, was a steel 452-foot steamer when she slipped beneath the surface of Lake Huron. During the White Hurricane the big ship was last seen heading north not far from Saginaw Bay. The ship disappeared with its cargo of coal and crew of twenty-eight.

On Lake Superior, the 472-foot steamer *L.C. Waldo* had taken on a cargo of iron ore on the western end of the lake. As the *Waldo* made its way through the storm, the ship was buffeted by high wind and waves. The captain of the *Waldo* was anxious to get behind the Keweenaw Peninsula to anchor in its shelter.

Blinded by the blizzard conditions, the *Waldo* misjudged its position and ran aground on Gull Island located between Passage Island and Keweenaw Point.

GREAT LAKES DISASTERS

The John A. McGean. *From the collection of the Port Huron Museum.*

The giant waves beat down on the stern of the grounded ship destroying its after deckhouse. The crew gathered in the bow awaiting rescue.

The Eagle Bay and Portage Life Saving Stations both made several attempts to get to the stricken vessel but were chased back by the storm.

The crew, hungry and cold, remained on the *Waldo* for four days while the waves crashed down on the ship before they were rescued.

The badly damaged ship was declared a total loss but was eventually removed, repaired and put back into service. Her career lasted another 54 years, sailing as the *Waldo*, *Riverton* and the *Mohawk Deer*.

During the Storm of 1913, the *Howard M. Hanna Jr.*, a 480-foot steel bulk freighter, was carrying a load of coal north on Lake Huron. The five-year-old ship passed the Huron Lightship as it entered the southern end of Lake Huron and passed into the history books as a ship that survived the Great Storm.

The *Hanna* worked its way north into the increasingly violent northeast storm while giant waves swept over the ship. Crewmen huddling in the after cabins listened to the terrible sounds of cables snapping, the screeching of metal being twisted and torn as the starboard lifeboats were ripped from their davits and the roof of the aft cabins blew off.

In the pilothouse, the helmsman and officers were not spared the storms savage fury. As the bow of the ship crashed into the monstrous waves, the pilothouse was pounded by the energy stored in the wall of water.

THE GREAT STORM OF 1913

The helmsman held onto the wheel for support as the ship at an almost 60 degree incline climbed the waves, when suddenly a wall of water crashed down on the ship, smashing the pilothouse windows and filling the pilothouse with cold Lake Huron water. Next the winds gusting to 90 miles per hour then tore off the roof of the pilothouse.

The *Hanna* was crossing Saginaw Bay when Captain Hagen wished he had sought the shelter at the government Harbor of Refuge at Harbor Beach, but there was no way he could turn back in the conditions.

As the tremendous waves crashed down on the *Hanna*, Captain Hagen found it impossible to keep the *ship* heading into the waves. Each wave crashing into the vessel pushed the bow to port, until the storm won the battle and the *Hanna* swung into the trough and became trapped broadside in the waves.

The ship now was subjected to a terrible pounding along its length. The ship rolled violently from port to starboard with the onslaught of each wave.

The wind and waves were so great the *Hanna* was pushed up on the rocky Port Austin Reef less than 1,000 feet east of the Port Austin Reef Light.

Stranded, the ship received the full brunt of the waves. Mountains of water smashed down onto the hapless ship tearing off all of her hatch covers and allowing thousands of gallons of lake water to pour into her hold.

Above the roar of the storm, the popping of rivets and the metal deck plates being ripped could be heard. The ship's hull was breaking apart.

The following day the seas and the storm subsided to the extent that some of the crew could take to the lifeboats and make it to shore. But, the *Hanna* was declared a total loss.

The Charles S. Price. *From the collection of the Port Huron Museum.*

The capsized hulk of a Great Lakes steamer was found floating in lower Lake Huron. From the State of Michigan Archives, Lansing, Michigan.

In the weeks and months that followed, salvager Tom Reid was able to re-float and rebuild the *Hanna* putting her back into service. The *Howard M. Hanna Jr.* survived the Great Storm of 1913 and sailed the Great Lakes for another 70 years!

The sinking of the 524-foot *Charles S. Price* was shocking to most mariners. How could such a large ship, just three years old, be sunk by a mere storm?

The *Price* was northbound with a cargo of coal, storm-warning flags flew and the storm was lashing the lake but the big new ship entered Lake Huron anyway. The Captain and crew had confidence in their ship.

The *Price* plowed into the wind and waves for almost 60 miles, to north of Harbor Beach, Michigan, when it is thought the *Price* tried to come about and return to the safety of the St. Clair River.

A large ship was later found floating bottom up in Lake Huron near Port Huron, Michigan. When the weather calmed, the Reid Wrecking and Towing Company tug *Sarnia City* went to the capsized hull. Lewis Meyers donned his hardhat diving suit and under the supervision of Tom Reid was lowered down to determine the name of the mystery vessel. He came up with the news; *Charles S. Price.*

The *Price*, only three-years-old, had "turned turtle" in the violent storm of November, 1913, a testament to the strength and fury of the storm. Her crew of 28 had perished in the disaster. In the following days their bodies began washing up on the Canadian shore.

THE GREAT STORM OF 1913

The James C. Carruthers. *From the collection of the Port Huron Museum.*

Also out in the storm was the sister ship of the *Price*, the *Isaac M. Scott*. The *Scott* at 524-feet in length and only four years old was steaming up Lake Huron with a load of coal. The ship fought for hours through the brunt of the storm until the "White Hurricane" finally got the best of the big ship. It's not known what happened, for there were not any witnesses left alive to tell, but the *Isaac M. Scott* went down with all twenty-eight crew about seven miles northeast of Thunder Bay.

The 545-foot, seven year old, *Henry B. Smith* had taken on a cargo of iron ore at Marquette, Michigan and on November 9th ventured out into stormy Lake Superior.

The captain of another ship docked at Marquette watched the *Henry B. Smith* attempting to turn around and return to the shelter of Marquette harbor. The *Smith* rolled violently in the seas and wind until she could no longer be seen through the blizzard.

The *Henry B. Smith* never returned to Marquette nor did it arrive at the Soo Locks. The ship never cleared Lake Superior. The *Smith* and her crew of twenty five went down in Lake Superior, north of Marquette.

The 550-foot *James C. Carruthers* was the largest ship to be lost in the Great Storm of 1913. The ship was also the newest, for the ship was in her first season on the lakes.

The huge ship was carrying over 10,000 tons of wheat when it is theorized that she was blown into the trough of the sea, was unable to recover and eventually succumbed to the horrendous storm. The big

THE PORT HURON TIMES-HERA

PAGE TWELVE

Bodies of Dead Washed on Shore Near Port Frank Are Robbed By Vultures As Sea Piles Them Up

Carruthers was later found off Kincardine, Ontario. The ship took her twenty five-man crew to their deaths.

It's hard to conceive that a mere storm could cause large ships to sink to the bottom, but the storm of 1913 is testament to the power of Mother Nature.

WHEN SHIPS COLLIDE: THE STORY OF THE LADY ELGIN

J. C. Herbert leaned on the railing of the *Lady Elgin* looking out into the night, listening to the splash, splash, splash sound of the paddlewheel turning in Lake Michigan. It was 2:00 am. He had been dancing and celebrating with the others in the salon, but he left to cool off on deck. It was a warm night, but the open deck was still cooler than it was on the dance floor in the forward cabin.

He reflected on the events of the day, a day that had already lasted some 20 hours. The Milwaukee Union Guard, one of Wisconsin's State Militia companies, left on the side-wheeler *Lady Elgin* during the early morning hours on September 7, 1860, arriving in Chicago at dawn. The hours were filled with a parade through the streets of Chicago, a tour of the city, a dinner dance, and a rousing speech from presidential candidate, Senior Illinois Senator Steven Douglas, who opposed a young lawyer also from Illinois, Abraham Lincoln.

Remembering the parade, J. C. thought to himself, what a sight we must have made. The Milwaukee City Band led the way, the brass and

The Lady Elgin *at dock. From the H. C. Inches collection of the Port Huron Museum.*

An 1860 drawing of the Lady Elgin. *Courtesy of the Wisconsin Marine Historical Society.*

drums announcing their arrival, followed by a procession of members of the Union Guard and guests. Next, the Milwaukee City Council, representatives of several of the cities' fire companies and a large number of Milwaukee policemen proudly waved to the gathered crowd. Wrapping up the spectacle was the Milwaukee Light Guard Drum Corps, always a favorite wherever they played.

He enjoyed the dinner and dance that followed, but his favorite memory of the evening was listening to Steven Douglas. J.C. and the Milwaukee Union Guard shared the beliefs of Senator Douglas. While they did not support slavery, they felt that it was the right of each state to determine if they wanted slavery. The Governor of Wisconsin did not share this belief. The Milwaukee Union Guard openly opposed the Governor. The Governor was so upset that one of the state's Militia would defy him that he ordered them to disband, revoked the Milwaukee Union Guard's charter and took back the Guard's weapons.

The Union Guard was determined to fight the Governor. They organized several fund raising events to purchase new weapons. One event was an excursion aboard the passenger ship *Lady Elgin* to Chicago.

The Guard would sell tickets for a boat excursion to listen to Senator Douglas and a portion of each ticket sold would be returned to the Union Guard.

The excursion was such a success that the ship was filled. The 252-foot long by 33.7-foot wide *Lady Elgin* was rated for 200 cabin and 100 deck passengers, but for this momentous trip there were many more than that.

WHEN SHIPS COLLIDE

The decks were lined with people, young and old, standing, sitting and sleeping wherever space could be found. The actual count of passengers on board the *Lady Elgin* that evening was estimated to be about 385.

The *Lady Elgin* had been built just 9 years earlier at Buffalo, New York. Her steam engine turned two paddlewheels, 32 feet in diameter, one on each side of the vessel. Known as a luxurious ship, she originally made the run from the eastern ports on Lake Ontario to Chicago but during the 1860 season, she ran primarily as a passenger and general freight boat up Lake Michigan to the Soo Locks, into Lake Superior and back.

J.C., staring absent-mindedly, was suddenly brought back to reality as the first flash of lightning lit the sky. Within seconds, a terrific crash of thunder followed. The rain came so hard it obscured visibility for but a few feet, and the waves grew, assaulting the starboard bow of the ship.

That morning the *Lady Elgin* was north of Chicago on the first leg of her normal route up Lake Michigan. The first stop was Milwaukee where the Union Guard would disembark.

The deck passengers, already pressed for space, scurried to find shelter from the rain. Mothers with babes in their arms, elderly and youth all trying to keep out of the rain and the wind. The main salon was filled with the Milwaukee Union Guard and guests. Although many had retired to their cabins, several still danced and reveled in the success of their day while the deck passengers huddled together attempting to stay dry.

Captain Wilson of the *Lady Elgin* had retired to his cabin. He could feel his ship being pounded by the seas and heard the wind mounting. He prepared to return to the bridge, knowing he may not be needed, but with the storm he felt more comfortable there. Before he could leave, he was knocked to the floor, books fell from a shelf and a glass crashed to the floor. The *Lady Elgin* had struck something, or something had struck it.

People dancing in the salon were thrown to the floor, several crushed against the wall by their friends as the ship took a sudden list to port. Those asleep in the cabins were awakened as their belongings flew from tables, and they were thrown from their beds.

Young Kenneth Cole, with his mother and a party of 15 others returning from eastern ports, was walking to his cabin when the ship took a tremendous lurch. He was thrown against the cabin wall, bouncing off a lady who had fallen. Blood ran down his face from the gash above his right eye.

Passengers on the decks, already panicked by the rain, thunder, lightning and heavy seas, now questioned the mysterious shudder and severe list to port.

GREAT LAKES DISASTERS

On the bridge of the *Lady Elgin*, the wheelman held the wheel tight, his knuckles white as he fought the force of wind and waves. Scanning the horizon through the rain and spray he saw something off the port bow. It disappeared in the rain, but then suddenly reappeared. It was a schooner sailing towards them.

The schooner, with its sails blown to tatters, and a severe list was blown by the storm on a collision course with the *Lady Elgin*!

Captain Darius Malott of the 128-foot, two mast schooner *Augusta* stood near the helm. The wheelman held tight to the wheel. The ship was blowing before the wind, not responding to the wheel.

The suddenness of the squall had not allowed the crew time to lower the sails. She was caught with a full head of sail with a gale force wind blowing down on her.

The deck load of lumber had shifted causing her to list drastically. Her canvas was being ripped to shreds as she was pushed with the wind.

Her foresail was blown out, removing her ability to maneuver; she was sailing out of control.

With no way to decrease the remaining sail area or to realign the deck load, the wind pushed her almost on her starboard rail. The storm was having its way with the schooner. She was sailing directly at the *Lady Elgin*, and there was nothing Captain Malott could do about it.

The *Lady Elgin*'s first mate saw the schooner appear out of the wind driven rain on a collision course with the paddlewheeler and screamed to the wheelman, "Port the wheel, port the wheel!" trying to get the *Lady Elgin* to starboard and allow the two ships to pass starboard to starboard, rather than port to port as was the rule.

Veins on his neck and muscles in his arms bulged as the *Augusta*'s wheelman fought the wind and seas to bring the ship to port to clear the paddlewheeler. The mate prayed his ship would turn and avoid a collision with the large steel vessel.

The wheelman and mate were violently thrown to the deck as the *Augusta* smashed into the port side of the *Lady Elgin*. The schooner's bow struck the side of the passenger ship just aft of the sidewheel, near the wheel box.

The schooner had pierced the *Lady Elgin* to the extent that its bowsprit penetrated deep into the *Elgin's* cabin work and was deeply embedded into her side.

The *Augusta* was dragged across the lake for several minutes with her bow buried in the side of the *Lady Elgin*.

WHEN SHIPS COLLIDE

The Lady Elgin *at dock. Courtesy of the Wisconsin Marine Historical Society.*

The forward motion of the *Lady Elgin* finally dislodged the *Augusta* but the schooners bowsprit pried the port paddlewheel off the passenger ship.

Panicking passengers onboard the over-crowded *Lady Elgin* ran in all directions, not knowing where safety laid. Adults, small children and the elderly unable to keep up were pushed down and trampled by the scared passengers.

People cried for life preservers. Unfortunately, there were just a few canvas vests with wood sewn into pockets, and passengers fought over them. The panicked lot screamed, cried, and prayed. Some injured lay moaning in pain. Others yelled for loved ones separated in the chaos. Above the human wailing could be heard the clanging of the ship's bell and the steam whistle sounding a distress signal into the night.

The frightened crowd on the *Lady Elgin* watched the schooner as it slowly broke away from the *Lady Elgin*. Over the howling wind a loud cracking of heavy timbers could be heard as the port paddlewheel was ripped away. The schooner with her sails still set caught the wind and the ship was being blown away from the crippled *Lady Elgin*.

Passengers on the *Lady Elgin* staring in disbelief, screamed for the schooner to stay and take them aboard, lower a small boat, or at least throw

A sketch of the Lady Elgin *slipping below at the stern with victims of the collision scatter about on the lake. Courtesy of the Wisconsin Marine Historical Society.*

over some of its deck load of lumber for them to use as floatation. Despite the cries from the *Lady Elgin*, the ship sailed off, disappearing into the rain and the dark of night.

Captain Wilson ran below to the engine room to survey the damage. His ship had sustained a large breach extending from just above the main deck to below the waterline. Cold Lake Michigan water was pouring into the ship.

Captain Wilson ordered the ship be lightened in hopes the breach in the hull could be raised above the water line. First to be thrown to the lake was the cargo of 50 head of cattle.

The cargo of heavy cast iron cook stoves was moved to the starboard side of the ship hoping to cause enough of a list to bring the port side gash above the waterline.

Crew in the engine room yelled to the panicking passengers above them to throw mattresses and other bedding down. They stuffed the breach in the hull hoping to slow the incoming water.

A ship's yawl was lowered with crew aboard to survey the damage and assist with filling the breach. The seas were so rough that the small boat was tossed about as if it were a cork.

WHEN SHIPS COLLIDE

As it approached the sinking *Lady Elgin*, the yawl was smashed against the hull. Crew attempted to fend the yawl off the ship with their oars, but as the waves pushed the small boat into the ship, the oars were snapped like twigs. The *Lady Elgin*, still under power, slowly pulled away from the yawl, leaving the crew to the mercy of the lake.

Returning to the bridge, Captain Wilson ordered the *Lady Elgin* towards shore. As long as the boilers produced steam, they would try to make it to the shallow water near shore.

The Captain turned to his first mate and confided, "Prepare yourself son, we won't make it to shore."

Aboard the *Augusta*, Captain Malott picked himself off the deck, where he had fallen as a result of the collision. He found his ship being dragged broadside by the larger passenger ship. He knew his wood schooner would not fare well in a collision with an iron hull vessel. As his ship dislodged from the *Lady Elgin* he heard the cracking and splintering of timbers and feared the *Augusta* was breaking apart. However what he heard was not his ship breaking up; it was the *Lady Elgin's* paddlewheel being ripped off by the *Augusta*.

As the *Augusta* dislodged from the passenger ship, Captain Malott feared the *Augusta* would soon sink. He thought the iron hull of the *Lady Elgin* had not sustained much damage and it would remain afloat. Captain Malott, ordered his ship to sail toward Chicago.

John Crilley and Charles Everts were asleep when the *Augusta* smashed into the *Lady Elgin*. They had retired to their cabin and quickly fallen asleep after dancing and indulging in merriment to celebrate the success of the day. The crash jarred them awake, almost throwing them to the floor. In their bedclothes, they left their cabin to see what had occurred. The ship had taken on such a list they had to climb uphill to get out of their cabin doorway.

"The ship is sinking!" came a cry from aft. Crilley froze in fright…he couldn't swim.

Charles Everts, running towards the main salon, yelled for John, "Come on, we need to find life jackets, and get off the ship!" John couldn't move, "No, I'll stay on the ship."

Charles ran back and grabbed John by the arm and pulled him into the salon. "The ship is sinking. You'll die if you stay!" Charles yelled at John.

No life preservers were found, so Charles began to remove cabin doors. "We can float on these," he reassured John.

GREAT LAKES DISASTERS

John, in a state of shock, took the door Charles handed him, holding on to it so tightly his knuckles whitened. He watched and listened to passengers on deck, running about and screaming. One woman clutching her baby to her breast screamed hysterically, "My baby, my baby!", while a man, face pale and eyes wide with fright slowly walked calling for his wife.

The two men, carrying their doors, joined the other panicked passengers in the main salon. Captain Wilson came in and shouted over the wailing crowd, "Get to the other side!" He yelled trying to keep the ship on a starboard list to raise the gash in the port side of the vessel above the waterline.

The *Lady Elgin*, black smoke bellowing from her stacks, headed towards shore. However, battling the seas, the wind, and the water pouring into her hull and with the port side paddlewheel missing, the ship made very slow headway.

Women screamed, babies cried and men huddled in panic in the main salon where they had earlier danced. Gaiety was replaced with fear. John, scared of the watery death which he was sure awaited him, clutched his door and prayed. Charles reassured him that they could make it to shore. "I'll carry you to shore on my back if I have to", he promised John.

Above the moaning and screams of the passengers, Captain Wilson ordered everyone to quickly go to the hurricane deck. There the crew was throwing overboard planks, doors, deck chairs and anything else that might float. Passengers reluctantly began to jump from the deck after the floats.

Charles yelled to John, "Follow me!" as he threw his door over and jumped in after it. Buoyed by the support of Charles, John held tight to the door as he jumped, fearing he would lose it if he threw it in. The door landed flat on the surface, John's face smashed into it on impact, breaking his nose and opening a gash in his forehead.

The damaged ship, creaking and twisting in the seas, was starting to break up. A metal strap supporting one of the smoke stacks broke in a metallic crack. The smoke stack crashed to the deck crushing several people huddled below.

Panicked all the more, mothers threw their children into the lake as people jumped from every deck of the ship. Moments later, the ship broke apart. The hull, filling with water, couldn't support the additional weight of the lake water and the *Lady Elgin* slipped below the waves at the stern, as her bow remained at the surface.

Hundreds of people still onboard were cast into the lake, some with life preservers, some with something to float on, many others with nothing. The screams of the victims, the howling wind and the thunder filled the night.

WHEN SHIPS COLLIDE

As the ship sank, a wood section of the cabin structure broke off and floated to the surface and a large section of the hurricane deck also surfaced. Scared men, women and children climbed on and laid across it, praying the raft would not break up in the heavy seas. Reaching out from the raft, others were pulled onto it. Women called out the names of their missing husbands and children, while they searched the violent lake and prayed they were safe.

The section of hurricane deck floated by Captain Wilson who was hanging onto a timber with one arm and holding an infant in the other. He handed the child aboard and climbed on. The piece of decking held over forty people. He settled and reached for the child.

Waves washed the raft, knocking people off. They frantically swam back to the raft and climbed on. Some weakened by the regular assaults of the sea couldn't regain the raft and slipped below the sea.

Captain Wilson handed the infant to a woman and stood to look for signs of the shore. As he reassured the people on the raft that they would safely reach the beach, a large wave broke down on the raft knocking the captain flat and washing the woman holding the baby off and she and the infant were lost in the churning sea.

John Crilley laid on his door, paddling as blood ran down his face. He yelled for Charles, who had given him the strength and courage to jump into the raging sea, but Charles was nowhere to be found. The door Charles had thrown over was there, but Charles was gone.

John paddled towards the sounds of people on a makeshift raft. He climbed on and hugged friends for support and warmth.

One of the yawls lowered by the *Lady Elgin* drifted towards shore, picking up eighteen men and women as they floated by them. The crew could hear the surf breaking on shore, they knew the worst wasn't over.

The small boat was being tossed and thrown in the heavy surf breaking on the rocks along the shore. Within sight of land, the boat was thrown end over end in the wild waves. The human cargo was cast into the sea; some washed up alive on the beach; others were killed as their bodies were pounded on the rocks.

The few that made it to shore found a cottage and woke the sleeping family. They survived the wild yawl ride and were made warm by the fire and fed.

Captain Wilson heard the breaking surf and knew their raft would be broken apart as it entered waves breaking in the shallow water. He prepared his fellow passengers for the peril that lay ahead of them. By this time the number on the raft had been decreased by the constant assault of the waves washing the tired and cold away.

The raft rose up on the crest of a wave, slipped back and the following wave crashed down on it washing all souls into the angry water. The waves smashed the raft into splinters. The human cargo cast into the water were thrown about by the seas breaking on the rocky coast. Some people were speared by the splinters of the raft. Some were picked up by the waves and thrown above the rocks to the safety of the beach. Others were smashed into the near shore rocks, their bodies broken and bloodied, while still others were pulled below the surface and drown.

Captain Wilson, who so bravely buoyed the spirits of those on the raft, never made it to shore. His battered body was recovered days later.

That night the *Lady Elgin* carried 385 passengers and crew. Only 98 lived through the night of horror, making it the worst disaster to occur on the Great Lakes up to that date.

The *Lady Elgin*
Music and words by Henry C. Work, 1861

Up from the poor man's cottage, up from the mansions door.
Sweeping across the waters, echoing along the shore.
Caught by the morning breezes, borne on the evening gale
Cometh the voice of mourning, a sad and solemn wail.

Chorus:
Lost on the *Lady Elgin*, sleeping to wake no more
Numbered with three hundred who failed to reach the shore.

Staunch was the noble steamer, precious the freight she bore
Gaily she loosed her cables a few short hours before
Grandly she swept the harbor, joyfully rang her bell
Little thought we are ere morning 'twould toll so sad a knell.

Chorus:
Lost on the *Lady Elgin*, sleeping to wake no more
Numbered with three hundred who failed to reach the shore.

Oh hear the cry of children weeping for parents gone
Children slept that morning, but orphans woke at dawn.
Sisters for brothers weeping, husbands for missing wives
Such were the ties dissevered by those three hundred lives.

Chorus:
Lost on the *Lady Elgin*, sleeping to wake no more
Numbered with three hundred who failed to reach the shore

THE MADMAN OF BATH, MICHIGAN

A tradition in American rural schools was the iconic one-room schoolhouse, a school where one teacher taught students of all grades with the older students helping teach the young. But in the early 1900s, a shift in educational thought was towards consolidating the one-room schoolhouses into one larger multi-grade building.

Experts of the time theorized students would receive a better, more thorough education if they were kept with students of the same age and educational needs.

The small town of Bath, Michigan, located about ten miles north of the state capital of Lansing was going through just such a transition. The school district in 1927 constructed a large two-story building to house all grades and closed several small rural schools.

In most small communities, the school was a source of pride. Almost everyone in the community had gone to the school, had children, grandchildren, nieces, nephews, or knew children attending. The school was the thread that held the community together.

As with most large and small communities, not everyone supported the larger school concept. It meant higher taxes for the community. And in 1927,

The Bath, Michigan consolidated school. From the Author's collection.

many in rural Michigan were still struggling after the 1920 stock market crash and the economic depression that followed.

The state of Michigan finances schools through property taxes and some people, especially the farmers who hold large tracks of land, were required to absorb a larger portion of the cost.

One man in the Bath Consolidated School District who was furious over the high cost of education was Andrew Kehoe. Andrew, together with his wife, owned a farm in the school district and despite making extra money with his ability to repair almost anything, he was having trouble meeting the mortgage payments on his property. He was in jeopardy of losing his land and home.

Andrew Kehoe was born in Tecumseh, Michigan, in 1872. After high school graduation, he attended Michigan State College in Lansing, Michigan for a while, then he decided to move west to Missouri where he enrolled in an electrical school.

While at the school, he fell from a ladder incurring a severe head injury. He laid in a coma for several weeks before regaining consciousness. After that experience, he moved back to Michigan and married his long time girlfriend, Nellie.

Andrew and Nellie purchased a 185-acre farm near Bath, Michigan, from the estate of Nellie's uncle.

Mr. Kehoe decided to run for the elected position of school board of the Bath District. His platform was one of fiscal responsibility and lowering taxes. He convinced enough people of his concerns to be elected in 1926.

Andrew was very vocal about the increased taxes levied to pay for the new school. In his mind, he blamed the school district for his financial distress. It was that damned new school that was putting a burden on him and causing him to lose his farm. He thought the district didn't need it in the first place; the old country schools were fine. It was the new building causing him to not make his payments to Nellie's aunt, and the family was breathing down his neck to pay or face foreclosure.

Kehoe especially blamed Emory E. Huyck for the higher taxes. Since Mr. Huyck became the superintendent of the Bath Schools, changes were made. Most thought the changes were needed. To Andrew the changes were unnecessary. They didn't need a new fancy building, and the curriculum had served the students for decades and was just fine. It didn't need changing. Andrew also thought Mr. Huyck spent a lot of money replacing equipment that was good enough for the children who had already passed through the school system.

To complicate his depressing financial situation, Nellie was having health problems that required frequent doctor appointments and expensive hospital stays.

Since Andrew could fix anything, when the school district needed a maintenance man, they hired Andrew. With his knowledge of electricity and anything mechanical, he was the best candidate.

Unfortunately, in the sick mind of Andrew Kehoe, he decided he would take care of his problems. He could fix anything and he would fix this, too. He would take care of the taxes, Nellie's health issues and her aunt nagging him about the farm payments.

As the maintenance man for the new Bath Consolidated School building, no one questioned why Kehoe was carrying boxes into the building or why he was stringing wire throughout the building.

On May 18, 1927, the last day of the school year, they found out how 55-year-old Andrew Kehoe was going to put an end to his problems.

The meticulous Andrew Kehoe started that morning at his farm. He bashed in Nellie's skull, killing her and putting an end to her expensive medical bills. He callously threw her lifeless body in an old cart and left it behind the hen house.

He sawed partway through the trunks of the fruit trees on the property and secured the animals so they could not escape. He gathered the scrap metal lying around the farm and piled it in the back of his pickup truck.

He had already constructed several homemade firebombs and placed them in each building on the farm. The house, barn, chicken coop, and all outbuildings contained a gasoline filled container with an automobile spark plug attached to it. The spark plug was wired into a battery.

Andrew Kehoe did one last thing. He carefully painted a sign and attached to the fence of his property. The words painted on the pine board were in Kehoe's mind a justification for the horror he was about to commit; "Criminals are made, not born."

At 8:45 on the morning of May 18, 1927, Andrew Kehoe detonated the bombs hidden on his farm. In a deafening blast, the Kehoe house and farm buildings exploded. Debris from the Kehoe farm was shot into the air and rained down as the house and outbuildings exploded in a huge fireball.

The animals trapped in the barn were burned alive, the fruit trees with their trunks sawn through toppled over, and the fires raged through the buildings. As Kehoe had planned, nothing would be left standing, everything would be destroyed. Nellie's aunt wouldn't get anything but the charred land.

Kehoe's neighbors came running towards the conflagration as he drove away in his pickup truck loaded with scrap metal.

A second explosion, larger and louder than had destroyed the Kehoe farm, was heard. The Bath Consolidated School blew up.

Andrew Kehoe, the school maintenance man, had spent months buying Pyrotol, a surplus World War I explosive similar to dynamite. He told the store clerk that he used the volatile chemical compound to blow tree stumps out of the ground. In actuality, he was placing it in vital locations around the school building and wiring the explosives with detonation devices. He had secretly hidden 1,000 pounds of Pyrotol in the rafters, between floor joists, and in the crawlspace, all connected by a mile of wiring.

The Bath school after the explosion. From the Author's collection.

THE MADMAN OF BATH, MICHIGAN

As he drove towards town, Andrew could see behind him his farm fully engulfed in flames. Ahead he could see a thick cloud of dust rising from the school.

At the sound of the explosion, people began running for the school. They were shocked to see the northwest wing of the building completely destroyed. The younger students, grades second through sixth, were housed in that section of the building.

Men and women dug through the rubble of the building to get to the children. Grown men sobbed as they lifted huge pieces of wood and concrete listening to screams, moans and cries of the injured children buried below. Arms and legs protruded from the piles of debris.

Firefighters and police from surrounding towns and villages and from the State capital of Lansing arrived on site after hearing the blast. Nobody was prepared for the death and carnage they found. Firemen carried the small-bloodied bodies of dead and injured children from the ruins of the building.

As rescue personnel carefully removed debris to get to the children trapped below, Kehoe parked his pickup truck and watched the commotion. He saw Superintendent Huyck and called him over to his truck. As the superintendent approached, Kehoe lifted a rifle, took aim at the homemade bomb in the truck and fired. The third explosion of the morning erupted. The scrap metal in the Kehoe truck and pieces of the truck were blasted hundreds of feet in all directions, hurling shrapnel in a killing path.

Superintendent Huyck was killed by the flying shrapnel as was Glen Smith, the town postmaster, standing nearby. Huyck was killed instantly and Postmaster Smith later died while his wife cradled his bloodied and dismembered body to comfort him. The blast also killed a 75-year-old retired farmer, Nelson McFarren.

Over one block away from the truck bomb when it exploded was Mrs. Perrone of Bath. Shrapnel struck her, ripping her eye from the socket and another projectile lacerated her scalp, penetrated her skull and punctured her brain.

The scrap metal truck bomb also ripped the body of Andrew Kehoe into unrecognizable pieces.

An inspection of the remains of the school found almost 500 pounds of unexploded Pyrotol and hundreds of feet of detonation wiring. The initial blast separated the wiring and resulted in only the Northwest wing of the building being destroyed. Had the explosion happened as Andrew Kehoe had planned, the entire building would have been destroyed, all classrooms, all grades and possibly the lives of hundreds of children.

Frantic Mothers Search Line At Morgue For Own Children

Tragic Melodrama Enacted As Women Lift Blankets From Tiny Forms Seeking Their Own Missing Children; Body of Arch Fiend Blown to Bits; Building Torn Apart By Blast Force

At the scene, parents joyfully reunited with their children while other mothers and fathers whose children had perished in the travesty, were comforted by friends and strangers.

The injured victims of the blast were removed to hospitals. The children and teachers killed in the blast were laid out in the school playground. Mothers and fathers frantically lifted the blankets covering the faces of the dead bodies looking for their missing children.

One family, Mr. and Mrs. Eugene Hart, discovered three of their five children had been killed in the explosion and the other two were hospitalized in critical condition. Four other families lost two children in the tragedy.

In the aftermath of the devastating bombing of the school it was found that 38 children were killed; one second grade student, ten from the third grade, seven fourth graders, six students of the fifth grade and thirteen sixth grade students.

In addition to the children injured and killed in the bombing, 21-year-old Hazel Weatherby, a third and fourth grade teacher in the Bath school district, was found dead in the rubble of the school cradling two of her students. Fifth grade teacher, Blanch Harte, was also killed as she taught her students.

Sixty-one others were injured in the explosion and carried the scars, both physically and mentally, for the rest of their lives.

The sick mind of Andrew Kehoe was responsible for the deadliest school killings in the United States. He planned and prepared for months to seek revenge for what he thought was an injustice. He blamed the Bath Consolidated School District and Superintendent Huyck for excessive taxes and the foreclosure on his farm. In his mind, the additional taxes for the new school is what took his farm and he was going to destroy the new school and the children within it.

CLEVELAND
EXPLOSION OF 1944

On October 20, 1944, on the east side of Cleveland, Ohio, Mrs. Bertha Ott and her youngest child were in their house when she heard a deafening explosion and everything in her house took on a red glow. She looked out the window and saw a horrific sight; the sky was filled with a wall of fire hundreds of feet high.

The grass in her yard was burning, her house was afire, and everything she could see was ablaze. She grabbed her youngest daughter, Geraldine, and ran from the house with only the clothes on their backs.

Mrs. Ott and Geraldine made it to safety; the other three Ott children were safe at school and Mr. Ott was at work far from the fire. But the Ott house and all of the family belongings, their three cats, "Tootsie" the dog and her puppies, and the Ott family chickens were killed in the blaze. They lost everything in the fire that swept over their neighborhood.

Not too far from the Ott house was the East Ohio Gas Company's natural gas storage facility where five large storage tanks held millions of cubic feet of natural gas. Three of the five tanks held natural gas, the other two contained liquefied natural gas.

Flames rise from the East Ohio Gas Company storage facility. Cleveland Press Collection, Cleveland State University Library.

Firefighters working to control the multiple fires. Cleveland Press Collection, Cleveland State University Library.

Liquefied natural gas is natural gas that has been refined by removing condensates such as water, oil, mud, as well as other gases. Liquefied natural gas takes up about 1/600 the volume of natural gas and can be more easily transported.

Today liquefied natural gas is commonplace but in 1944 the process of converting natural gas was in its infancy. The East Ohio Gas Company facility in Cleveland was only the second storage facility in the United States.

The two storage tanks each designed to hold 90 million cubic feet of liquefied gas, were built in 1941, during World War II. Most of the steel production of America was used in the war effort so the tanks were made of a lesser quality alloy. The alloy contained much less nickel making it susceptible to fatigue from low temperatures.

On the fateful day of Friday, October 29, 1944, the liquefied natural gas started to leak from a seam of tank #4.

CLEVELAND EXPLOSION OF 1944

The colorless and odorless liquefied natural gas turned to a vapor when it mixed with air. The white vapor floated from the tank and was blown on an onshore breeze from nearby Lake Erie. The vapor seeping from the tank went unnoticed. The white haze crept along the curbs of streets, some of it entering buildings and some entering the sewer system through the catch basins.

The highly volatile gas seeped into houses through drains, as it traveled through the mixed residential and light industrial neighborhood though the sewers.

At approximately 2:30 pm, the liquefied natural gas tank ignited resulting in a tremendous explosion, blowing fragments of the storage tank and the flames from the burning gas hundreds of feet in the air. The shockwaves from the blast shattered windows for several hundred feet around.

The flames followed the escaping gas into buildings turning them into a conflagration of intense heat. The gas in the sewers was also ignited and a ball of flames raced through the sewers. When the flames reached a location where a high concentration of gas had accumulated, a tremendous blast resulted. Manhole covers were blown from the streets; one was found over a quarter mile away.

People ran from their homes in a panic. Some, like Mrs. Ott and Geraldine, ran from their burning homes. The volatile gas had crept in and

Scene from the East Ohio Gas Company storage facility after the explosion. Cleveland Press Collection, Cleveland State University Library.

The aftermath of the explosion and fires. Cleveland Press Collection, Cleveland State University Library.

ignited. Others ran from their homes at the sound of the explosion but found their home had been saved from the catastrophe; some never had a chance to run, and they were incinerated by the blaze.

Twenty minutes later the second tank containing liquefied natural gas exploded from the intense heat of the fire. The blast threw a shower of shrapnel from the tank in all directions and another shaft of flames rocketed into the sky.

The flames shot out igniting homes that survived the first blast of fire. The people who thought they had been spared, found themselves in an inferno of epic proportions.

Many of the employees of the East Ohio Gas Company working at the storage facility were killed instantly when the explosion and resulting fire engulfed the tanks.

In seconds, one square mile of East Cleveland, bounded by St. Clair Ave. NE, E. 55th St., E. 67th St., and the Memorial Shoreway, was engulfed in a sea of fire as explosions ripped through the neighborhood.

The flames consumed almost everything in its path. Seventy-nine homes and two factories were destroyed. Miles of underground sewers were ruined, 217 cars, one semi-truck and seven trailers were reduced to smoldering, unrecognizable heaps of metal.

Over seven hundred people were left homeless. More than two hundred people sought medical treatment from burns and other injuries and one hundred and thirty one men, women, and children were killed by the explosions and resulting inferno.

The area was evacuated and the residents were taken to a shelter at Wilson Jr. High School. There the Red Cross set up army cots and provided food and drink for the refugees.

The East Ohio Gas Company was quick to settle with the families of their employees and those of the residents killed in the blasts.

The Cleveland gas explosion led to improvements in handling and processing natural gas. New methods were developed for the construction of storage tanks. New materials were developed for storage tanks that were capable of handling the extreme low temperatures of natural and liquefied natural gas.

One improvement was that natural gas is colorless and odorless making a leak hard to detect before the gas meets a source of ignition and explodes. The Federal government passed a law requiring an odorant, thiophane, be added during processing to give the gas a foul smelling rotten egg odor making it easier to tell if there is a leak.

THE CHERRY MINE DISASTER

In the early years of the twentieth century, coal mining was considered one of the most dangerous occupations in America. The men and boys who worked underground in the mines lived in constant fear of injury or death.

The work was grueling. The miners toiled in narrow, dark, dank tunnels, often working several hundred feet below the surface. And the threats against the lives of the miners were many; explosions, fire, toxic gases, being trapped by a cave-in, and the possibility of drowning in a mine flood.

Mining companies gave little thought to the safety of the worker. If a miner didn't like the conditions he could leave; there were many men in the flood of immigrants that were moving to America that were eager to take their place.

In 1909, coal was in demand to power the steam locomotives that were the primary form of transportation of the day. The geographic location of Chicago in the Midwest made the thriving city a hub for railroads. Most rail traffic heading east or west across the country stopped in Chicago.

In 1905, the Chicago, Milwaukee, and St. Paul Railroad invested in the St. Paul Coal Company mine in Cherry, Illinois, to supply coal for their trains. Cherry is located just a few miles northwest of La Salle, Illinois, and about 90 miles from Chicago. The small town in the heart of the Northern Illinois coalfields was on the St. Paul rail line that could take the coal directly to Chicago to the rail yards.

The St. Paul Mine in Cherry was one of the most modern in Illinois, if not the world. On the surface, eleven buildings made up the mine complex. There was a main office, an emergency hospital with a full time physician, a powerhouse, brick engine room for the two Lichfield hoisting engines which lifted the cages on 1-3/8 inch cables. The engine room also housed the dynamo to generate electricity. There was another engine room, a brick boiler house with six boilers to produce steam to operate the engines, a machine shop, a storage building, carpenter shop, blacksmith house and the vital fan house with its sixteen foot diameter fan blades that blew fresh air down into the mine.

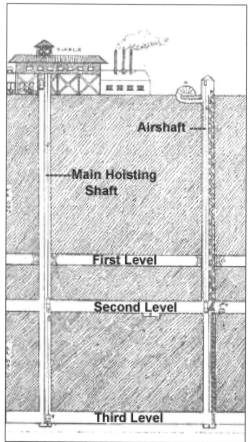

At the opening of the main shaft stood a 92 foot tall iron tower that lifted two, 6 foot by 16 foot steel cages. The cages operated alternately, one rising while the other descended.

The hoist cages were pulled to the surface with the coal cars and its valuable cargo. The coal was dumped into the hopper, weighed and sorted, then the coal was dumped into a railroad hopper car below.

Below ground there were three levels. At the first level the coal vein was found to be too narrow to be of any commercial importance. By 1909, most of the mining was done on the second and third level. The second was 315 feet down and the third 500 feet below the surface.

The main shaft was sunk to the 500 foot level but the hoist cage only descended to the second level. The air-shaft, located 350 feet from the main shaft, went down to the 500 foot depth.

Illustration from: the State of Illinois Bureau of Labor Statistics, "The Cherry Mine Disaster," Library of the University of Illinois Urbana-Champaign, Springfield, Illinois, 1910.

At the second level there was a corridor running east and west from the hoisting or main shaft. That corridor, running 300 feet in each direction, was 12 feet high and 16 feet wide.

Oak timbers were erected to support the walls and heavy wood boards were fitted along the roof of the corridor to prevent rocks and dirt from falling on the miners below.

Two sets of tracks were laid along the bottom for the coal cars to run. The coal cars were small wooden carts, six feet long and three feet wide with iron gears and railroad wheels pulled by mules.

THE CHERRY MINE DISASTER

The scene of the disaster at the St. Paul Mine in Cherry, Illinois.

At the second level there was a 20-foot long and 10-foot high pump room where a state of the art pump was housed to remove excess water seepage from the mine. There was also a room large enough to stable 55 mules.

The entire 600-foot length of the second level, the pump room and stable were lighted by electric lights. Very few mines in the country were equipped with electric lights; most were lit by torches and by the light on the miners hats.

At the second level there were corridors branching off in all directions for over a quarter of a mile following the vein of coal. In the corridors branching off the main, the miners would shovel the coal into a train of six coal cars and a team of three mules would pull the train to the hoist shaft where two cars at a time were lifted to the surface in a steel cage.

Coal from the third level was hoisted to the second through the air shaft. Then the cars were pulled through the corridor to the main shaft to be hoisted to the surface.

A set of stairs were built in the main shaft. The wooden stairs zig-zagged up the side of the shafts in case an emergency forced the miners to exit and the hoist was somehow incapacitated.

On the morning of November 13, 1909, 481 men and boys went down into the mine for the day's work. They started descending down on the hoist between 6:30 and 7:00 am and began work on both the second and third levels.

Two weeks prior, the main electrical cable providing light underground was doused with ground water and shorted the circuit. A new cable was ordered to replace it but it had not been delivered as of November 13. So for two weeks the mine was lit by kerosene torches hung on the timbers that supported the walls. The torches were actually two lengths of pipe each 16 inches long. One end of the pipes was capped off to hold the kerosene and the other end held a cotton wick. The pipes hung on the timbers. When they began to dim, the capped end of the pipe was tipped up to send the kerosene to the wick.

Normal quitting time was 3:30 in the afternoon but because it was a Saturday, several miners quit early and caught the 1:30 cage to be hoisted to the surface. The miners were paid by the tons of coal they dug, not by the hour, so hundreds of others remained in the mine to earn more money.

At any time there were between sixty and seventy mules in the mine working the second and third levels. At least once a day bales of hay were loaded into the empty coal cars at the surface and lowered into the mine. The cars loaded with hay for the third level were pulled by mules to the other end of the mine to the air shaft where they would be lowered to the third level.

On November 13, a coal car with six bales of hay standing on end was lowered down the main shaft. The car and five others were pulled by a team of three mules near the air shaft where the team was unhitched and used to pull a train of cars loaded with coal and rock back to the hoist shaft.

Robert Deans and fifteen year old Matt Francesco pushed the car with the bales of hay by hand closer to the shaft, then walked away. Unfortunately, the car with the bales of hay came to rest directly below a kerosene torch.

Kerosene leaked from the capped end of the torch and the bales of hay soaked it up like a sponge.

A bit of the burning wick apparently dropped into the bale and a fire erupted. Miners attempted to move the coal car but it resulted in spreading the blaze. The timbers supporting the walls and the roof boards ignited. Even the vein of coal caught fire and burned with toxic black smoke.

The burning coal car filled with its flammable cargo of kerosene soaked hay was shoved down the air shaft to the third level where there was a six-foot deep, water filled sump. The sump and two men at the third level with a hose extinguished the blazing coal car. But the second level was ablaze.

THE CHERRY MINE DISASTER

The remains of the fan house of the St. Paul Mine.

When word of the thick smoke was heard at the surface, the engineers decided they should reverse the direction of the air shaft fan. Instead of blowing fresh air down the air shaft, they wanted to suck the smoke out of the mine. They thought it would be best for the miners trapped below.

Twelve men volunteered to go down into the mine to warn the miners and help them to escape the fire. The volunteer crew consisted of the mine manager John Bundy, and assistant manager Alex Norberg. Six miners, a cageman, a liveryman, a grocer, a driver, a clothier also volunteered.

As the crew was lowered down the main shaft, they found that the fire burning at the other end of the mine was burning its way towards the main shaft. The rescuers found the mine becoming more inhospitable; the smoke was suffocating with almost zero visibility. The men felt their way around and yelled for lost miners.

The twelve rescuers had made arrangements with the hoist operator prior to going down: three bells meant the hoist operator was to start pulling the cage up; if there were four bells, the operator was to pull up slowly, and other such commands.

The twelve heroes descended into the inferno to save the men and boys trapped below seven times and succeeded in bringing several miners back to the surface.

Each time they were lowered, their wives and loved ones pleaded with them not to go down again, but the men knew they had to go down, the lives of hundreds of men rested in their hands.

The hoist operator heard one bell signal from below. That was not one of the signals agreed on. In the confusion he did not raise the cage. He waited several minutes before deciding to pull the cage up.

The relatives of the twelve screamed in horror as the cage broke the surface. All twelve of the rescuers were dead. Their clothing was still on fire and they were laying in grotesque positions, their burnt hands across their faces in a failed attempt to block their faces from the intense heat. Eight men laid in the bottom of the cage while four had climbed to the top of the cage trying to escape the inferno.

When the sixteen-foot diameter fan was stopped and slowly started up in reverse, the fan began to suck the smoke, heat and flames up the air shaft. The fire shot up the airshaft cutting off the only way for the miners on the third level to get to the second level. The fire shooting up the airshaft destroyed the fan and ignited the air shaft house on the surface.

The following day two men with masks and oxygen tanks strapped on their back were lowered down the air shaft in a makeshift bucket. They were able to be lowered to the second level but found the smoke and heat too great to explore the area.

Both the air shaft and the main shaft were capped to hopefully smother the fire in the mine.

By Monday November 15th, two days after the fire started, the fan was repaired and again turned on in reverse. A group of rescue miners descended the main shaft but were turned away by the flames. The fan sucking air from the mine and the opening of the main shaft proved to provide oxygen to the flames that had diminished. The fire erupted again into a blaze.

Both shafts were again covered.

It wasn't until Thursday, November 18, when the temperature at the second level was low enough for firemen from Chicago, equipped with oxygen tanks, to enter the mine and fight the fire with hoses lowered from the surface.

Eight days after the underground blaze was under control, it was safe enough to allow workers into the mine to look for bodies.

The exploratory team was sent out to search the second level and its side corridors for their fallen comrades. Their progress was hampered by several cave-ins that they had to dig through. But their efforts were rewarded when they found 21 miners still alive!

A photograph showing the conditions the men and boys working in coal mines endured.

The 21 had made their way to a short side corridor off the main. They built a wall of wood, mud and rocks to separate themselves from the smoke, flames and poisonous gases permeating the mine.

The men were rushed to the surface and to the hospital. All but one survived.

The men and boys later related their story of their entombment in the mine. Miner George Eddy took the lead and gathered all the miners he could find together and attempted to find a way out of the mine. After one of the men died of asphyxiation, the miners decided their only salvation would lie in finding a cavern with safe air to breath and to wall themselves off from the fire, smoke and gas.

They had no food and only the water they found by digging into the floor of the cavern and finding a small spring. They spent their days in despair and prayer, and wrote letters to the loved ones whom they never expected to see again. The trapped miners had light for four days before

GREAT LAKES DISASTERS

the kerosene burned out leaving them in total darkness. On the last day of their captivity, the men decided that they couldn't remain any longer and that four of the men who were the strongest would venture out of the cavern and see if they could make it to the main hoisting shaft. That is when they walked into the crew searching for the bodies of dead miners.

Finding men and boys alive seven days after the fire began renewed hope for the wives, mothers, fathers and children of the men lost in the mine. Unfortunately, no other miners were found alive.

On November 13, 1909, two hundred and fifty nine men and boys were killed in the St. Paul Mine. The mine built with all of the latest innovations fell victim to the failure of one of the innovations, the electric lights. Had the lights been functioning properly, kerosene torches would not have been in use.

The fire was the indirect result of the electrical cable being short-circuited and requiring replacement. Ironically, the replacement cable arrived at the mine the morning of the fire.

The owners of the St. Paul Mine were found guilty of, and paid a small token fine, for violating the child labor laws by hiring boys under the mandatory age of eighteen. Several of the miners killed and many of those who were able to escape were much less than 18 years old.

As a result of the disaster that killed 259 men and boys, the Illinois legislature enacted the first workers compensation program in the United States. The United States Bureau of Mines was established to inspect mines and enforce better and safer mining practices.

S.S. EASTLAND: THE WORST DISASTER ON THE GREAT LAKES

On the morning of July 24, 1915, Mrs. Grochwska, her daughter Kitty, and Kitty's friend, Rose Moldt, were standing in a mass of people waiting to board the huge white steamship, *S.S. Eastland*. Kitty, 18 years old, and Rose, 19, were excited, looking forward to a fun day at the Western Electric's employee picnic.

The girls giggled as they pointed out good-looking young men they saw in the crowd. Mrs. Grochwska playfully scolded the girls, then pointed out a man off to their left. The girls were giddy with anticipation of what the day would bring. They didn't know that in just a short time they would become victims of the worst shipping disaster ever to occur on the Great Lakes.

The *S.S. Eastland* was one of the five excursion ships chartered by the Western Electric Company for their annual employees' picnic. The ships

The Eastland *as she looked in years before her accident.* From the collection of the Eastland *Disaster Historical Society.*

were docked on the Chicago River amid thousands of people anxious to board. The 256 foot *Eastland* would be the first to board.

Over seven thousand tickets had been sold for the event, and the crowd assembled on the wharf early to get on one of the first ships to leave.

The trip aboard the *Eastland* to Michigan City's Washington Park would depart at 7:30 AM. Passengers began lining up long before that in hopes of being on the *Eastland*. It would be the first ship to load and depart, and it was the fastest of the five ships hired for the day.

Passengers poured through the gangways, and most ran up the grand stairway to the top decks where they could line the starboard rail to wave and yell to their friends. The ship began to take on a slight list to starboard which is normal when passengers gather dockside prior to departure.

An order was given from the bridge to the engine room to steady the ship. Valves were opened, and river water began to flow into the port ballast tanks. The ship righted as the water's weight countered the weight of the passengers at the starboard rail.

Listing while loading was nothing unusual for a passenger ship. On a freighter, the cargo is carefully loaded and positioned to prevent the ship from becoming unstable. Yet on a passenger ship the human cargo does not evenly distribute their weight on the ship, in fact the people are a mobile cargo that results in the ship constantly needing to be trimmed. Typically, as they board, large groups of passengers gather along one side and the ship needs to take on or pump out ballast to compensate.

Kitty and Rose, on the top deck of the Eastland, waved their handkerchiefs and shouted to friends on the dock, feeling special that they were lucky enough to board the first ship, the luxurious and

THE WORST DISASTER ON THE GREAT LAKES

Passengers lined the wharf waiting to board one of the five ships chartered by the Western Electric Company for their annual employee's picnic. From the collection of the Eastland *Disaster Historical Society.*

fast *Eastland*. They would be the first to depart and first to arrive at the picnic.

A ship's officer walked by asking passengers to move to the other side but the girls, like the rest of the passengers, stayed by the dockside rail.

Before long, the *Eastland* began to list to port, even though the largest congregation of passengers lined the starboard rail.

Again, the Captain called the engine room with orders to take measures to compensate for the list. Below decks, ballast water was pumped from the port tanks and the ship slowly shifted back to an even keel.

2,500 passengers, the maximum amount the *Eastland* was certified to carry in 1913, had boarded the ship. Those waiting on the dock were diverted to the next ships, the *Theodore Roosevelt* and the *Petoskey*.

The *Eastland* began to again list to port.

Captain Pedersen gave the order to prepare for immediate departure even though the ship remained unstable with a very noticeable list to port.

Kitty and Rose heard Bradfield's Orchestra begin to play on the deck below them. They looked at one another, a wide-eyed smile came across their faces and without a word, ran from the rail and raced below decks towards the music.

The *Eastland* continued with a list to port. Some passengers noticed the angle of the ship as they walked, but few were concerned.

The more experienced crew was very concerned. In the engine room, men frantically worked the valves to the ballast system, trying to right the

The S.S. Eastland *before gaining fame as the ship which killed more people on the Great Lakes than any other. From the H.C. Inches Collection of the Port Huron Museum.*

ship. As the stern line was released, the aft end of the ship drifted out into the river. The listing grew to the extent that water began to pour in through the port gangways and scuppers. The bilge pumps were started.

Captain Pedersen felt if he could get the ship out of the river into the open water of Lake Michigan, he could better deal with the problem. He called for a tug to escort the *Eastland* and asked for the drawbridge to be opened. The bridge master refused to open the bridge fearing the ship was too unsteady to get underway.

The list to port of the ship dramatically increased as its stern floated free and the bow remained tied to the dock. Passengers began to scream as they could no longer ignore the list and began to slide across the decks towards the port side. Dishes could be heard breaking in the kitchen as they tumbled from the shelves.

Kitty and Rose had pushed their way into the main salon towards the music but could not reach the dance floor due to the huge crowd already there. They leaned against the port cabin wall as the list increased. Passengers in the main salon began to scream. The fun of the day turned to terror. The two girls reached for one another and hugged, trying to fight off fear.

Passengers ran as best they could to the deck in panic. Kitty screamed as she saw the piano rolling across the dance floor increasing in speed as it rolled on the inclined surface of the floor. The piano narrowly missed hitting several passengers as it crashed into the port wall.

Tables and chairs slid towards the port wall, pinning people. Kitty and Rose both screamed at the sound of the bar refrigerator crashing to the floor. The large heavy refrigerator slid across the floor. Passengers frantically tried to escape it until it crashed against the cabin wall, crushing Kitty and Rose.

Water poured in port gangways while the boiler stokers, in a panic, climbed the ladder to escape a certain death as the water rose in the boiler. The bilge pumps, already working, were no match for the incoming water.

The orchestra had braced themselves as best they could and played, trying to calm the passengers, until their chairs slid out from under them. The music stopped and was replaced with the shrieks of the frightened and panicked aboard. Passengers above and below deck clung to the starboard rail and anything nearby to prevent themselves from sliding to port.

On the main deck, passengers crawled toward the stairwells attempting to save themselves. Others on the main deck jumped from the ship off the starboard side. Some made the leap to the dock and some landed in the river.

As more water poured in through the gangways, the list worsened. Suddenly, without hesitation, the *Eastland* rolled onto her port, coming to

The tug Kenosha *forms a bridge for survivors to evacuate the* Eastland *just after the accident. From the H.C. Inches Collection of the Port Huron Museum.*

rest on the river bottom, her starboard hull exposed. The list had become too great for the ballast tanks to compensate.

Those on the open decks were thrown from the ship into the river. A survivor of the disaster, Harlan Babcock, described the scene: "In an instant, the surface of the river was black with struggling, crying, frightened, drowning humanity. Infants floated about like corks."

The ship, almost 40-feet in beam, settled to the bottom of the 20-foot deep river. The river's surface became alive with hundreds of bobbing heads screaming for help. Many, unable to swim or too scared, succumbed quickly to the river. Others looked to the thousands still lining the docks and screamed for help.

Passengers aboard the other ships looked on in horror as their friends, just moments before happy and gay with the anticipation of the day's events, died before their eyes. A lifeboat and life rafts from the *Eastland* floated free but floated empty in the sea of drowning *Eastland* passengers and crew.

Life preservers, deck chairs, and anything that would float was thrown to the screaming throngs in the water. Lifeboats were hurriedly lowered

The Eastland *lies near the wharf while hundreds of dead are brought from the interior of the ship. From the collection of the* Eastland *Disaster Historical Society.*

THE WORST DISASTER ON THE GREAT LAKES

The Eastland *lies on her portside resting on the river bottom. Rescue vessels are seen assisting in the recovery of the hundreds of souls who died that morning.* From the collection of the Eastland *Disaster Historical Society.*

from nearby ships. Many victims were taken aboard, but the immensity of the disaster was so great that many of the passengers cast into the river were overcome by panic and shock and died in the water.

Harlan Babcock continued, "I shall also never forget the way those wailing, shrieking women -and some men - clung to the upper railings of the capsized boat. In mad desperation they grasped the rail, knowing that to let go meant possible death."

Those on the open decks who were cast into the river were the lucky ones. Many passengers were trapped below decks. Those in cabins on the port side were drowned as the ship rolled over and filled with river water.

The unfortunate souls who were along the port salon walls were crushed by the weight of others thrown against them as the ship overturned. Cries came from the mass of humanity stacked several deep. Some tried to claw out of the mass of carnage. Several bodies were later found to be scratched and gouged by people trapped under them. The water crept up, slowly drowning those not killed by the weight of the others. Soon the screams and cries for help subsided as the passengers drowned within the confines of the ship.

Passengers trying to climb the grand stairway were crushed when the stairway collapsed under the weight of the crowd. Those who were not killed in the fall were trapped, their means of escape lay in a tangled heap of wood, metal, flesh and blood.

Many others were trapped in cabins, passageways, or other areas with no means of escape, screaming for help as the water rose. They drew in a deep breath as the water neared their heads, only to involuntarily exhale and suck in river water, filling their lungs to die an agonizing death.

Families huddled together, nowhere to go as water crept up around them. Fathers and mothers held their children high to no avail as the water rose. Families died together. Many children, mothers and fathers were later found locked in a deadly embrace. Twenty-two entire families were killed on the fateful morning.

Some trapped below decks had to step on the bodies of their dead friends as they tried to find a way to escape death. Portholes on the starboard side were opened, and those small enough to fit through climbed out to join the passengers and crew who had made it to safety.

A fireman holds the lifeless body of an infant pulled from the wreckage. His expression speaks to the horror of the day. From the collection of the Eastland *Disaster Historical Society.*

THE WORST DISASTER ON THE GREAT LAKES

From the collection of the Eastland *Disaster Historical Society.*

Several passengers who had staterooms onboard the ship were trapped when the ship overturned. They were killed when they were unable to exit though the damaged or blocked cabin doors. Groups of the dead were later found floating, trapped in their cabins.

Some passengers lucky enough to be close to a starboard gangway door were able to climb or be pulled to the side of the vessel lying above the river's surface. Rescuers reached down into the gangways to the mass of people climbing on one another trying to escape the ship. Many were pulled to safety while others were crushed by the panicked.

Hundreds stood on the starboard side of the ship, shaken, many in shock but alive.

The Chicago Police and Fire Departments were quick to respond to the capsizing. Tugs and other boats nearby steamed to the area. Dead bodies were pushed aside to gain access to those still alive, floundering in the river. Several people from the crowd on the wharf dove into the river to rescue those in the screaming mass.

Some victims reached out for anything that could save them; life preservers and furniture thrown from the other ships and wood ripped from the wharf. Some of the panicked grabbed other passengers and drowned them in an attempt to save themselves.

The tug *Kenosha* was now pulling passengers from the river. "Save those who can be saved!" cried the captain as dead were ignored and only those moving were pulled to safety. Some men openly cried as they used pike poles to push away floating bodies to reach those showing life.

Pounding from inside the hull could be heard by rescuers and survivors standing on the starboard hull. The trapped pounded and scratched at the hull, hoping someone would hear their signal and rescue them. Firemen on the starboard side of the ship used their axes on the wood cabin structure to release passengers trapped inside. Soon men arrived with cutting torches to cut holes in the *Eastland's* steel side.

Captain Pedersen and his first mate ran to them, demanding they stop. He didn't want anything done to harm the integrity of the ship's hull. Several of his men tried to help the captain prevent holes being cut into the hull but were arrested.

The torches cut large holes in the starboard hull, allowing many to escape. Rescue workers jumped in through the holes and pulled the injured to safety. Rescue workers in the hull waded in chest high water, feeling with their feet for the bodies of the dead.

Hardhat divers were summoned. They dove in the water in the ship with the grim task of bringing out the bodies of those trapped below decks.

The dead, by the hundreds, were brought out of the ship and river during the day and into the night. A temporary morgue was set up in the nearby Second Regiment Armory. Bodies covered with sheets were carried on stretchers to the Armory. The stretchers were quickly emptied and rushed back to the scene of horror to be filled again.

From the collection of the Eastland *Disaster Historical Society.*

THE WORST DISASTER ON THE GREAT LAKES

The bodies of the hundreds of passengers killed on the Eastland *were taken to the Second Regiment Armory and lined up for the identification by the next of kin. From the H.C. Inches Collection of the Port Huron Museum.*

"A woman who was one of those rescued from the upper railing stood weeping at the top of the pier," said Harlan Babcock. "When she stepped onto the *Eastland* an hour before, she had her husband and little boy."

"Whenever a child's body would be brought to the street, she would wildly demand to see the face. Finally, a tiny form was brought up, and before police could stop her, she grabbed the body and pulled the blanket away from the cold white face of the child. It was her baby and she fainted."

Rescue workers and the hundreds of people lining the river's edge watching the catastrophe unfold before their eyes were haunted by the painful screams of the people trapped below decks. Soon they were haunted by the silence when the screams stopped.

The joyful chatter of the passengers as they boarded was replaced with cries for help, then tears for the dead. On that fateful morning of July 24, 1915, 815 people died as the *Eastland* rolled over to port.

In the days that followed the capsizing of the *Eastland*, an investigation into the cause of the greatest marine disaster ever to occur in the Great Lakes began. Sailors familiar with the vessel recounted she was widely known as a "tender" ship, meaning she was prone to listing.

The investigation revealed that in her first year, just months after her maiden voyage, the *Eastland* took on such a list that lake water poured in

The Eastland *lies on the bottom of the river as the wrecking tug* Favorite *prepares to right her. From the H.C. Inches Collection of the Port Huron Museum.*

through her gangways. The following year, while returning from South Haven, Michigan, with a cargo of over 3000 passengers, the ship began to take a precarious list to port. The engineers over-compensated, and the ship then listed precariously to starboard before she was brought steady.

The listing was of such concern the passenger capacity of the *Eastland* was reduced from 3,300 to 2,800. In 1906, after another listing scare, the capacity was lowered yet again to 2,400. However, the capacity was later raised to 2,570, the amount of passengers and crew aboard the *Eastland* on July 24, 1915.

The *Eastland*, launched in 1903, was designed to transport passengers and cargo on the lucrative route between Chicago and South Haven, Michigan, and other west Michigan resort areas. The cargo she primarily hauled was fruit grown in the South Haven area to the ready market of Chicago.

The specific cargo and ports of call required the ship be built to certain specifications. The Black River at South Haven was only about 12 feet deep, so the ship had to have a shallow draft; also, the ship needed to be fast. These two requirements would be found to have an effect on the stability of the ship. Simply stated, there was too much weight above the water line and not enough below. The ship was top heavy.

THE WORST DISASTER ON THE GREAT LAKES

To counter the listing, the ship was equipped with a ballast system to take on lake water into either the port or starboard tanks to help stabilize the ship, but the system proved to be inadequate. The tanks could not be filled nor emptied quickly. Another problem was the ballast intake port was the same used to pump the ballast water out, making it impossible to empty one tank while the tanks on the other side were filling. The ballast system would not allow water from one tank to be shifted to the other.

The newspapers, through either sensationalism or a lack of facts, projected that over 1,800 deaths would result from this tragedy. It was later lowered to just over 900, but most modern day projections agree that 812 souls met their death that day.

The dead were not the only ones to suffer. Thousands of Chicago residents lost relatives. Thousands more on the dock and other excursion ships and rescue workers had to live the rest of their lives with the screams echoing in their dreams.

In the days and months that followed the tragedy, many allegations of wrong doing against the captain, officers and the ship's management were made. Indictments were made, grand juries were called and civil suits were brought.

The S.S. Eastland *once again afloat. The ship still wearing a coat of Chicago River bottom mud. From the H.C. Inches Collection of the Port Huron Museum.*

The Eastland *after the accident was sold and renamed the* Wilmette.
From the collection of the Michigan Maritime Museum.

The *Eastland* remained lying on the bottom of the Chicago River while salvage crews made repairs to the ship in preparation of righting her. On August 14, 1915, the ship was righted and moved to a nearby shipyard for repairs. The ship never sailed again under the name of the *Eastland*. She was sold at auction for $46,000 and eventually retrofitted as the *Wilmette*, an Illinois Naval Reserve training ship. The ship served until 1947 when it was cut up for its scrap value.

No other shipwreck on the Great Lakes has come near to the level of human loss as the *Eastland* disaster. Ironically, the ship was still tied to the dock.

CENTRALIA COAL MINE DISASTER

On the afternoon of March 25, 1944, nearly a thousand residents of the small south central Illinois town of Centralia gathered at the Centralia Coal Mine. They awaited word of the their friends and loved ones who were 540 feet below the surface in the Centralia #4 mine.

Just before quitting time, around 3:30 pm, the day shift was ending and the afternoon shift preparing to begin their workday. The afternoon shift on the surface heard a rumbling and saw a dirty gray plume emit from the air shaft of the mine. The men knew something was wrong. An accident had occurred in the mine.

The Centralia Coal Co., owners of the Centralia Mine Number 5, had been mining the area since 1907. They employed 259 men to work in the mine that covered almost six square miles underground. Over the years the mine had flourished, producing 2,000 tons of coal per day.

But, the mine was not without problems. Driscoll Scanlan was a mine inspector for the Illinois Department of Mines and Minerals and on several occasions inspected the Centralia Mine Number 5. In his reports he indicated that the mine was dirty and dusty, and noted a buildup of coal dust on the roadbed, walls and timbers of the mine.

An inspector for the United States Bureau of Mines also toured the mine and found similar conditions. The report of the federal inspector called the mine, "Highly explosive."

Scanlan inspected the Centralia Mine Number 5 again in December of 1944 and found conditions had not improved and recommended that the mine be closed until the explosive coal dust was cleaned up.

In 1945, there were yet more violations of safety standards. In April the mine was closed for three days at the insistence of the Bureau of Mines. By June an inspection revealed that conditions had again deteriorated to a near critical situation.

Also in 1945, the United Mine Workers Association, Local 52 brought up charges against the Centralia Mine Number 5 manager that he permitted an explosive to be discharged while men were working in the mine. The company admitted that it had done so but for emergency reasons and that it would not happen again.

In November of 1946, another inspection by the United States Bureau of Mines was made. A letter was sent to the Centralia Mines Company instructing them that they must correct all of the violations found. The company responded that they could not due to the miners strike which was occurring.

In January of 1947, the Bureau of mines instructed the company to correct all hazardous conditions by February. The company, in February, wrote back informing the Bureau that many hazards were corrected. The Bureau wrote back asking for details.

Two of the most dangerous conditions that existed in the mine were a lack of adequate ventilation and the layer of fine coal dust on the roadways. The dust was highly combustible and had to be either cleaned up or covered with a sufficient amount of rock dust. A layer of rock dust prevents the coal dust from becoming airborne and prone to explosion. The Centralia Mine did not comply with standards and did not apply rock dust where it was necessary.

In March of 1947, just days after the last correspondences between the Centralia Mine Company and the United States Bureau of Mines, there was an explosion in the mine.

As the men were preparing for the end of their shift and to rise to the surface, there was a deafening explosion. The company was blasting away overburden, material that covered the coal seam. The blast occurred in violation of the policy that stated that blasting cannot be done while miners were in the mine.

However it was a common practice of the Centralia Mine to have the same men who drilled the shot holes be the same ones to fire the shots. This was normally done at the end of the shift while the miners were leaving the mine.

The blast ignited the excessive amount of fine coal dust in the mine and the dust exploded in a flash fire. Miners in the vicinity of the blast were killed instantly, burned beyond recognition. Other miners died a choking and suffocating death from breathing afterdamp.

Afterdamp is the toxic mixture of chemicals following a coal dust explosion, the most deadly of which is carbon monoxide that kills by depriving victims of oxygen.

The miners at the surface sounded the alarm whistle at the sound of the explosion and the sight of the dark gray plume of smoke rising from the air shaft. Wives, mothers, fathers and children all knew what the alarm meant; there was an accident in the mine.

In the small community, everyone knew the 142 men trapped in the mine. People sobbed, prayed, and begged for information on the miners.

It was quitting time so several miners were in the hoist shaft being lifted to the surface. They had only traveled 40 or 50 feet when the explosion rumbled through the mine.

John Pick, Jr. was one of the men going to the surface. He was thrown to the floor by the explosion, rendering him unconscious for a short time. When he came to, all was dark and the air was filled with choking rock and coal dust. The men in the hoistshaft were in a state of confusion, they asked what had happened, how were the other men, would they begin to suffer from the afterdamp, had they seen their last day?

John Pick Jr. wondered about his father. They had gone down the shaft together that morning. The last words his father, John Sr., said was; "So long, Jack. See you at quitting time." Now he didn't know where his father was or if he was alive or dead.

John says he must have passed out because the next thing he remembered was waking up on the surface.

As soon as the emergency alarm sounded, miners who were part of a trained rescue team gathered at the mine. The men quickly put on their equipment and descended the 540 foot shaft. With masks and breathing from the oxygen tanks strapped on their backs, the men slowly moved through the dust filled main corridor in search of miners who had survived the blast.

Doctors, nurses and the Red Cross reported to the mine ready to lend assistance if they were needed.

The rescue team proceeded very slowly in the dark and gas filled four-mile long corridor. The dust was so thick the men could only see a few feet ahead. When they came to a side corridor they searched for survivors then boarded up the entrance to the side corridor, pumped fresh air in to force the carbon monoxide out. Then they walked another 60 feet to the next side corridor and repeated the process.

As the rescue team searched, they came across several bodies of miners who did not survive the blast. It was hard for the men to find a miner's body and pass it up. The dead were not of importance; they were searching for men still alive.

A crowd estimated at 1,000 gathered at the mine head waiting for news of the miners still trapped below. They hoped the men had found a corridor free of carbon monoxide where they could shelter until help arrived.

Mrs. Mary Pawliss sat in shock, waiting for word of her 22-year old son, Jack, who worked the mine. She prayed he used the survival training he received in the Navy, had found a safe gas free place or that he remembered what his grandfather had told him.

Jack's grandfather had twice been in a coal dust explosion. He told his grandson he survived by digging a hole in the dust and breathing carefully the air in the hole.

Jack's father who also works in the mine was sick that morning and did not go to work. Mrs. Pawliss was thankful that at least she did not have to worry about both of them.

A map of the mine provided by the company showed that some of the miners were working almost four miles from the area the explosion occurred. Those miners might have had time to construct a temporary wall to block off the poison gases.

Hours passed and the rescue crew came up from the mine only finding eight miners alive. The rest of the miners had not survived the blast and resulting gases. The rescue crew's mission changed from rescue to a body recovery.

The crowd gathered at the mine thinned as wives, children, mothers and fathers of the miners returned to their homes to grieve their loss.

Bodies of the miners were brought to the surface and taken to a makeshift morgue. Burns and the shock wave from the explosion killed sixty-five of the miners. Their bodies were badly contorted and showed signs of severe trauma from the explosion. Another forty-five of the miners died as a result of afterdamp.

Twenty-four of the miners were close enough to the hoist shaft that they were able to escape from the mine without assistance. Eight men were found alive in the mine and brought to the surface by the rescue crew, one of the eight later died from injuries he sustained in the blast.

One hundred and forty two miners descended into the Centralia Mine Company's Number 5 mine on March 25, 1947. They lived in constant fear of death from cave-ins, from explosions and from toxic gases. Over the next two days 111 of the miners were brought back to the surface to be buried.

In the days and months that followed the tragic and preventable deaths of the Centralia miners, John L. Lewis, United Mine Workers Association President inspected the mine where the worst mining accident since the Cherry Mine disaster occurred. He vowed that he would fight for reform and safer working conditions for the miners of the United States.

CENTRALIA COAL MINE DISASTER

United Mine Workers Association President John Lewis returning from the depths of the Centralia Mine.

In his testimony before congress Mr. Lewis proclaimed:

"If we must grind up human flesh and bone in the industrial machine we call modern America, then before God assert that those who consume coal and who benefit from that service because we live in comfort, we owe protection to those men first, and we owe security to their families if they die."

John Lewis was successful in his attempt to sway the federal legislature. Congress took up the fight and legislated enforceable standards for mining companies.

Woody Guthrie wrote the following song shortly after the disaster at the Centralia Mine:

"The Dying Miner"

It happened an hour ago,
Way down in this tunnel of coal,
Gas caught fire from somebody's lamp.
And the miners are choking in smoke.

Goodbye to Dickie and Honey,
Goodbye to the wife that I love.
Lot of these men not coming home,
Tonight when the work whistle blows.

Dear sisters and brothers goodbye,
Dear mother and father goodbye.
My fingers are weak and I cannot write,
Goodbye Centralia, goodbye.

GREAT LAKES DISASTERS

It looks like the end for me,
And all of my buddies I see.
We're all writing letters to children we love,
Please carry our word to our wives.

We found a little place in the air,
Crawled and dug ourselves here.
But the smoke is bad and the fumes coming in,
And the gas is burning my eyes.

Dear sisters and brothers goodbye,
Dear mother and father goodbye.
My fingers are weak and I cannot write,
Goodbye Centralia, goodbye.

Forgive me for the things I done wrong,
I love you lots more than you know.
When the night whistle blows and I don't come home,
Do all that you can to help mom.

I can hear the moans and groans,
More than a hundred good men.
Just work and fight and try to see,
That this never happens again.

Dear sisters and brothers goodbye,
Dear mother and father goodbye.
My fingers are weak and I cannot write,
Goodbye Centralia, goodbye.

My eyes are blinded with fumes,
But it sounds like the men are all gone,
'Cept Joe Valentini, Fred Gussler and George,
Trapped down in this hell hole of fire.

Please name our new baby Joe,
So he'll grow up like big Joe.
He'll work and he'll fight and he'll fix up the mines,
So fire can't kill daddy no more.

Dear sisters and brothers goodbye,
Dear mother and father goodbye.
My fingers are weak and I cannot write,
Goodbye Centralia, goodbye

HAMMOND CIRCUS TRAIN DISASTER

Joe Coyle had been a circus clown for several years and still absolutely loved it. Joe loved the thrill of the circus; the horses, elephants and exotic animals, the performers, the excitement of the audience, the aroma of popcorn and cotton candy wafting through the midway, the hawkers walking through the audience selling tasty treats to the children and the sound of the air calliope and its melodic tones. He loved the look of amazement on the faces of the children as the bareback riders did their stunts on beautiful steeds prancing around the ring, the laughter of the crowd as the clowns performed, the deep baritone voice of the ringmaster announcing the acts, the big top and the gaily-painted circus wagons were all the heart and soul of Joe's life.

Joe was working with the Hagenbeck and Wallace Circus. In 1918, it was the second largest circus in America. He appreciated the tradition of the Hagenbeck and Wallace Circus performers for he was chief clown in a circus that was once home to such great clown performers as Joe Skelton, father of Red Skelton and America's most loved clown Emmett Kelly.

On Friday June 21, 1918, the circus was performing two shows in Michigan City, Indiana. Joe dressed in his signature costume; oversized baggy white pants which were way too short, huge floppy shoes that made a flapping sound when he walked, an oversized white coat with gigantic black buttons worn over a black and white striped shirt, and a large white and black-striped hat. His face was painted white with exaggerated eyebrows and bright red lips.

Joe did a routine with several other clowns, entertained the audience while other acts performed and did a comic bicycle act in the Grand Parade.

Since Joe's wife, infant son and two year old son were traveling with the show for a little while, his two-year-old son, Joe Junior, was dressed in a clown costume and billed as the "Youngest Clown in the United States."

The Hagenbeck and Wallace Circus was a large traveling show, second only to the Ringling Brothers and Barnum and Bailey Circus. Audiences throughout the Midwest were thrilled by the Hagenbeck and Wallace show

Circus elephants, one of the biggest crowd pleasers, performing under the big top. Photograph from Wiki Commons.

which featured the "Flying Wards," an extremely popular trapeze act, Strongmen Max Freehand and brothers Art and Joe Dericks entertained the crowds with feats of superhuman strength. The show even advertised a ballet show featuring 100 dancers.

Horses played a large part in the show. The exquisite bareback riding of the beautiful Louise Cottrell from London, England, was always a crowd favorite wherever the circus performed. There was a precision equestrian group. A husband and wife team, The Bartletts, showed off their skills at riding bucking broncos, and the "Wild West" show featured wagons pulled by four horse teams and drivers firing their six shooters in the air.

The circus was home to all types of exotic animals, their trainers and those who tended to the animals. Gigantic elephants performed stunts and paraded under the Big Top. The lions and tigers in the big cage with a lion tamer cracking a whip and staving off the ferocious animals with a chair were always a favorite.

Outside along the midway, the sideshow grinders or talkers would try to lure the townspeople into buying a ticket to the sideshow tent where they would see all kinds or wild and exotic acts, two headed cows, Siamese twins joined at the head, the bearded woman, the half man/half woman, the child covered with hair and a number of other strange and unusual acts.

HAMMOND CIRCUS TRAIN DISASTER

When the Michigan City show closed, the animals, show cages and circus wagons were loaded onto the first of two circus trains the Hagenbeck and Wallace show used. The performers and roustabouts (workers who set up and tore down the circus) broke down the big top, sideshow tent and midway and loaded it on the second train.

Once the lot was cleared, the almost 400 performers and crew boarded the second train and went to their Pullman cars at the rear of the train. The last four cars, just ahead of the caboose, were old wood Pullman cars converted for the circus's use. They were brightly and gaudily painted in reds, yellows and emblazoned with gold lettering. The arrival of the circus train in a town was almost as anticipated as the show itself.

The old Pullman cars had been remodeled. The interior of the cars were rebuilt with berths three high on each side of the car, the berths slept two to a bunk. Management saw this as the best use of space. Most of the people on the train were in the four cars at the end of the train.

The train traveled overnight to their next stop at Hammond, Indiana, where they would set up at Calumet Avenue and 150th street. The circus would set up the big top there to entertain the throngs of adults and children.

The first train with the animals and their cages and circus wagons arrived at Hammond and was busy getting ready to move the animals and equipment from the rail yard to the circus site.

Moving the equipment from the rail yard to the show site was done as a parade of gaily-painted wagons arrived along with the brightly painted horse drawn wagons containing the lions, other big cats, and elephants.

The second train departed Michigan City with the big top and most of the performers and roustabouts. They would arrive the following day and set up again.

About 4:00 in the morning, a conductor aboard the second train detected a hot box on one of the flat bed cars. A hot box is a bearing box on a rail car's wheel truck that has lost its lubrication and is over heating due to friction. If the bearing is not repaired it could seize and cause a fire or derailment.

Just east of the Hammond city limits, in Ivanhoe, Indiana, the engineer of the 26-car second circus train pulled onto a sidetrack to allow the conductor to check the over-heated bearing box.

Most of the 26-car train, made up of fourteen flatcars, seven animals cars, four sleeper cars and a caboose was on the sidetrack except the caboose and the four Pullman sleeper cars remained on the main track.

Following protocol, the circus train dropped off a flagman, Oscar Timm, to switch a warning semaphore a mile behind the rear of the train.

A Hagenbeck and Wallace Circus Car. Courtesy of the Durand Union Station, Michigan Railroad History Museum.

He also set a warning flag a quarter of a mile from the train still partially on the track. A brakeman from the circus train fired several red burning fuses (flares) and placed them between the rails to warn any oncoming trains that the track was not clear.

Two block signals were automatically set indicating the track was not available, two red light signals had been set by the flagman as a warning, and several red fuses burned brightly between the tracks at the rear of the circus train, so any oncoming train should be warned that the circus train had not cleared the track.

Alonzo Sargent had worked with the Michigan Central Railroad Company for almost 30 years, the last 16 as a locomotive engineer. He was assigned to take a train of twenty Pullman cars from Kalamazoo, Michigan, to the rail yard at Chicago, Illinois. The train had taken a load of army troops to Kalamazoo the day before and was returning empty.

Engineer Sargent had followed a freight train to Michigan City where he pulled onto a sidetrack to take on water. Sargent's empty troop train departed the water tower and was made aware of a circus train on the track ahead of them. He had to slow down a few times when signals indicated the circus train had slowed.

At the East Gary, Indiana, rail yard, Engineer Sargent slowed to about 25 miles per hour to comply with yard rules. And after clearing the yard, the troop train accelerated once again to sixty miles per hour.

HAMMOND CIRCUS TRAIN DISASTER

As the troop train with Alonzo Sargent at the controls was steaming, the engineer said he had an open track with no warning signals.

Circus train flagman, Oscar Timm, was nearly a half of a mile from the rear of the circus train standing at the side of the tracks with his red lantern. He looked east and saw the headlight of a locomotive in the distance. The train should have stopped; the automatic signals had been switched to red, the semaphore signals were set, but yet the train seemed to be advancing at an alarming speed.

Timm watched in amazement; the train shouldn't have been on the track as it wasn't clear. And it certainly should not have been running so fast; didn't the engineer see the warnings?

Oscar Timm kept waiting for the steam engine to start braking. However it kept speeding towards him. The flagman furiously swung his red lantern back and forth yet the train didn't stop; it didn't even slow.

He didn't see anyone in the engine. Thinking the engineer was asleep, Oscar threw his lantern into the open window of the troop train engine as a last ditch effort to wake the engineer and avert a train wreck.

The engine continued at sixty miles per hour speeding towards the caboose and Pullman cars that remained on the track.

With a huge crash, the locomotive of the troop train smashed into the caboose of the circus train destroying it in seconds. The momentum of the

The locomotive of the Michigan Central Railroad troop train, which collided with the Hagenbeck-Wallace Circus train.

locomotive carried it into the next three cars. The old wood Pullman cars were split up the middle from the impact. The performers and roustabouts sleeping two to a berth, three berths high were crushed as the steam locomotive of the troop train plowed through the cars.

The kerosene lamps in the Pullman cars were smashed and spewed flames catching the remains of the wood cars on fire. Some of the people sleeping in their berths that weren't killed by the impact of the accident were burned to death in the fire.

The wreckage was strewn on either side of the tracks piled up as high as the telegraph wires and flames leaping high in the air.

The fire kept anyone from getting close enough to rescue those in the train. All they could do was stand off from the blazing debris and listen to the screams and cries of those trapped inside.

When firefighters responded, they found there was no water to use to extinguish the fire. Water had to be trucked in.

At 4:00 in the morning on June 22, 1918, eighty-six people were killed and 127 were injured. Most of the dead were from the caboose and four Pullman cars. There were very few people who escaped from the wreckage of that part of the circus train.

The aftermath of the Hagenbeck-Wallace Circus Train accident showing the total destruction of the last four cars of the train.

HAMMOND CIRCUS TRAIN DISASTER

The Chicago Sunday Tribune. FINAL EDITION

THE WORLD'S GREATEST NEWSPAPER

VOLUME XXVII—NO. 25.   JUNE 30, 1918.   PRICE SEVEN CENTS

ARREST WRECK ENGINEER

FIREMAN ALSO MUST EXPLAIN
61 CIRCUS DEAD

Whole families of performers were killed; some of the dead included "The Flying Wards," who were devastated with the death or serious injury of five of their troupe. The Derick Brothers, the strongmen, were both killed, and the wife and two infant sons of clown Joe Coyle were killed. Yet, Joe who was with them was uninjured.

Joe's wife and youngest son were pulled from the wreckage of the sleeper cars. Their bodies were taken to the morgue in Gary, Indiana. Joe remained at the site of the collision looking for his other son.

The charred body of the "Youngest Clown in the United States" was later pulled from the debris to the morgue to lie with his mother and brother.

The engineer of the troop train, Alonzo Sargent, had run through an automatic caution signal located a mile back from the caboose of the circus train, a semaphore warning, the flagman's lantern and several red burning fuses placed between the rails.

Sargent and the fireman of the troop train walked away from the accident and hopped aboard a train taking the injured to a hospital in Gary. From there they took a train to Kalamazoo, the Michigan Central Railroad divisional headquarters.

Sargent at first claimed that he had not seen any of the warnings because they were obscured by the steam of a passing steam engine. But he later admitted that he was indeed asleep in the engine. The cause of the catastrophe, the reason 86 people lost their lives, the reason for the 127 injured was an engineer asleep on the job.

The engineer and fireman from the Michigan Central troop train were arrested and charged with manslaughter. The charges against the fireman were dropped but Alonzo Sargent was transported to Hammond, Indiana, to face the charges.

Many of the dead were burned beyond recognition and were buried in Woodlawn Cemetery in Forest Park, Illinois. A section of 750 burial plots called "Showman's Rest" had recently been set-aside to bury men and

83

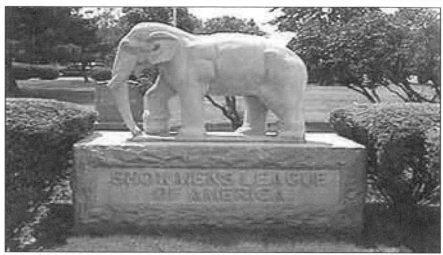

The central Showman's Rest monument. Photograph from the Wikipedia Commons collection.

woman from the theatrical arts. Between 56 and 61 of the dead of the Hammond Circus train are interred there.

The "Showman's Rest" section is bordered on the corners with small elephant statues and a larger elephant with its trunk in a lowered position which indicates it is in mourning.

> *"There will be no circus in Hammond this year.*
> *The kids will get left this time." Unidentified*
> *Hagenbeck and Wallace Circus Clown.*

Wallace Brothers train wreck at Durand, Michigan

The 1918 accident wasn't the first railroad accident the circus had been involved in. In 1903, two Wallace Brothers trains collided at the Durand, Michigan, rail yard.

The circus had preformed in Charlotte, Michigan, and the first of the two-train assembly consisting of a locomotive, tender and 21 cars, departed about midnight in route to Lapeer, Michigan. The second train, by rules of the railroad, was required to stay a half hour behind.

About 3:00 in the morning the first circus train came to a stop about a half of a mile from the Durand yard. A stock train ahead of it had stopped to investigate a hot box.

HAMMOND CIRCUS TRAIN DISASTER

As per railroad regulations, a flagman hung a red lantern on the caboose and walked three quarters of a mile from the rear of the circus train and lit a red warning signal. Red fuses were also lit behind the first circus train to warn the oncoming second circus train.

The second 17 car Wallace circus train had engineer C. M. Propst at the throttle, and fireman, H. E. Colter and William Benedict, the train's brakeman in the engine. As the train rounded a gentle curve in the early morning darkness they saw the red warning lights of the train blocking the main track.

With plenty of distance to stop, engineer Propst reached for the air brake lever. He applied the brakes but nothing happened and the train did not slow. The brakes had been used when the train stopped to take on water at Lansing so they should be working now.

He reversed the lever and applied the brakes again, holding the lever tightly in hopes that they would activate and slow the train.

When it became apparent that the second section of the circus train was not going to stop, the engineer told the fireman and brakeman to jump! Propst tried the lever once again in desperation and when nothing happened, he too jumped from the engine just moments from impact.

The morning quiet was suddenly shattered when the locomotive, running at least 20 miles per hour, some say much faster, smashed into the rear of the first circus train.

The engine drove into the caboose and somersaulted, coming to a stop upside down in a ditch near the shattered remains of the last two cars of the number one train.

Railroad employees slept in the caboose. The next car was a coach car that housed circus roustabouts and performers. The third car contained animals and trainers.

Citizens of Durand, awakened by the horrendous crash and the fire whistle, quickly dressed and ran to the carnage near the Durand rail yard. They were horrified to see the mangled heap of wreckage. They heard the hissing of steam escaping from the engine, the screams and moans of people trapped in the debris and the roar of the lions, tigers and other circus animals. They saw bloodied corpses, and arms and legs torn from bodies everywhere they looked.

Townspeople, railroad workers and circus employees began to extract the bodies from the mangled remains of the train, some dead, some barely alive, some wandering aimlessly in shock.

Asleep in the caboose were J. W. McCarthy, Trainmaster, Special Officer of the Grand Trunk Railroad, A. W. Lange and J. Foley, the foreman

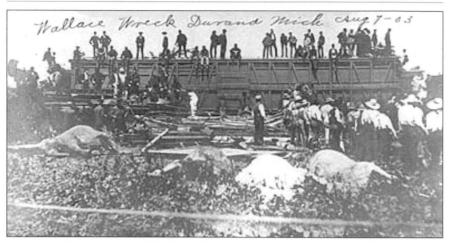

The wreckage of the 1903 circus train accident at Durand, Michigan.
Courtesy of the Durand Union Station, Michigan Railroad History Museum.

of locomotives. The first two were killed instantly when the engine tore through their rail car. Mr. Lange was severely injured and later died.

The coach car was the quarters of the canvas crew whose job it was to raise and lower the big top and sideshow tents. Most of men in the car were killed in the impact of the engine smashing through the caboose and the coach car.

In the third car were the circus elephants and camels and their trainers. Maud the elephant, two camels and a highly prized performing bloodhound were killed along with several of the animal handlers. Several of the animals were thrown on top of Jip, a large elephant who was injured in the accident.

Animal trainers rushed to the remaining animal cars fearing the lions and tigers had escaped and were roaming the countryside, but the menagerie were still caged and remarkably calm despite the crash.

In all, 24 were killed in the accident. Most of those were killed at the first impact and were in the second to last car. The majority were canvas men, ring stock handlers, horse drivers in the wild west show and the harness maker and blacksmith.

There were hundreds of men and women injured in the collision. Broken and crushed arms and legs, lacerations on the torso and face, brain concussions, skull fractures, sprained or broken backs, burns and internal injuries were some of the injuries that required hospitalization, while others were treated at the scene for less serious wounds.

HAMMOND CIRCUS TRAIN DISASTER

The dead were taken to a temporary morgue and laid in rows for the next of kin to identify. For days, people from around the country came to walk the rows of the dead looking for brothers, husbands and sons. All but ten were identified and taken home for burial. The remaining ten were buried in Lovejoy Cemetery in Durand.

The Circus
by
Red Skelton
A tribute to his circus clown father, Joe Skelton.

The circus! The magical city
That appears and disappears
With the bat of an eye.
A cathedral for children and adults
Made of canvas and trimmed with red wagons.

A sunburst of wheel, pink lemonade and cotton candy.
A temple housing the unity of man and beast...
All performing for the good of their fellow man
With shouts of glory.

The performers' only reward is the echo of the applause
And laughter of children
It cradles them to sleep,
As the red wagons roll from city to city.

A lesson in humanity,
Where man and beast risk life and limb
For the meager reward of applause.
How sad it would be if my youth would pass away
And not see the beauty of the big red wagons
And taste the rare vintage of pink lemonade!

Oh, keep me young
Without prejudices, without haste,
So that I will be young,
So that my heart will be filled with glee
Next year, when the big red wagons roll in again!

THE CRASH OF UNITED AIRLINES BOEING 247

A United Airlines Boeing 247 Transcontinental propeller airliner departed Newark, New Jersey, October 10, 1933, with a final destination of Oakland, California. There were several stops en route; the first was at Cleveland, Ohio, where the plane took on fuel and mail. The next scheduled stop was Chicago, Illinois but the plane never made it that far. The United Airlines Boeing 247 with a tail number of NC13304 exploded and crashed to the ground.

A Boeing 247D was one of the most modern airplanes of its time. The airplane entered service in 1933 as the first airliner to have an all metal fuselage, landing gear that retracted into the body of the airplane. The Boeing 274D also was equipped with automatic pilot and two-way radio communications.

In 1933 the Boeing aircraft company built 76 aircraft, seventy of which went into service for the United Airlines. The two Pratt & Whitney S1H1-G Wasp 550 hp engines powered the aircraft at cruising speed of 188 miles per hour with a maximum ceiling of 25,387 feet.

The Boeing 247 had accommodations for 10 passengers, with improvements in passenger comfort. Soundproofing was installed in the cabin, there was a lavatory in the cabin, air vents and reading lights for each passenger and thermostatically controlled heating and cooling.

On October 10, 1933, on the leg from Cleveland to Chicago there were only four passengers; 25 year old Fred Schendorf of Chicago, 15 year old Dorothy Dwyer of Massachusetts, K. Smith of Chicago, Illinois, and Warren Burris from Columbus, Ohio.

At the controls of the Boeing 247 were pilot Harold Tarrant, and co-pilot A. T. Ruby both from Oak Park, Illinois. Aboard the flight to accommodate to passengers was stewardess, 26-year-old Alice Seribner from Chicago.

The flight was on schedule and the pilot reported that all was well. Suddenly at 8:46 pm while the plane was 50 miles southeast of Chicago, flying at an altitude of 1,000 feet, an explosion ripped through the Boeing 247.

GREAT LAKES DISASTERS

A Boeing 247 on the tarmac. From the NASA photographic collection.

Residents about 5 miles from Chesterton, Indiana, heard the explosion and looked up to see an airplane on fire and gyrating erratically towards the ground, crashing into a wooded area with a second explosion and a huge ball of fire shooting up several hundred feet into the night sky. The tail section of the aircraft was ripped from the fuselage in the initial explosion and landed nearly a mile from the main crash site.

All persons aboard, passengers, pilots and the stewardess, were killed.

Investigators quickly responded to the crash site to search for a reason for the accident. The aircraft was brand new, not quite two months old, the pilots were experienced and competent, and United Airlines had not had a fatal accident in 40 million miles.

The engines were inspected and found to be working normally at the time of the explosion and the fuel tanks were damaged but did not show signs of an explosion.

Further research by the United States Bureau of Investigation under the direction of Melvin Purvis, head of the Chicago office, produced some perplexing evidence. The baggage compartment and the lavatory were more severely damaged than the rest of the aircraft. Those sections were blown into shreds while the rest of the plane only displayed damage from the ground impact and resulting explosion. Another interesting discovery was that the interior of the lavatory door had been penetrated by hundreds of chards of metal while the cabin side of the door showed no such damage.

The evidence led the investigators to believe the aircraft was brought down by an explosive devise in the baggage compartment at the rear of the aircraft. The forensics further showed that everything in front of the baggage compartment showed signs of being blown forward and everything behind the compartment was blown towards the rear.

THE CRASH OF UNITED AIRLINES BOEING 247

Wreckage of the aircraft was taken to the Crime Detection Laboratory at Northwestern University. The experts there, with the cooperation of the Porter County coroner's office, determined the crash of the Boeing 247 aircraft was the result of an explosive device, possibly containing nitroglycerin, being detonated while the aircraft was in flight.

The practically new United Airlines Boeing, equipped with state of the art technology, had fallen from the sky after a bomb exploded ripping the tail assembly from the aircraft.

The downing of the United Airlines Boeing 247 was the first proven act of sabotage on a commercial airliner. Another macabre first was that Stewardess Alice Scribner, a licensed nurse in her first month on the job, was the first United Airlines flight attendant to be killed in a plane crash.

The United States Bureau of Investigation turned their attention from determining the cause of the airplane craft to determining who was responsible for blowing up the United Airlines airplane.

Their investigation went in many directions. There were reports of a passenger who took a package wrapped in brown paper aboard the aircraft. The mysterious package seemed like the likely source of the explosion but when it was found in the wreckage still intact it was ruled out and the passenger who took it aboard was no more of a suspect than the others in the aircraft.

They investigated the rifle that was found in the wreckage, but it was owned by a passenger who was flying to Chicago to compete in a competition at the Chicago North Shore Gun Club.

Baggage handlers at Newark, New Jersey, and Cleveland were interviewed but no one with access to the baggage compartment proved to be a person of interest. There was no reason for the passengers or crew to detonate an explosive on the airplane. All leads the Bureau investigated went nowhere.

To this day there has not been anyone charged or convicted of the October 10, 1933, bombing of the United Airlines Boeing 247 over Chesterton, Indiana; the first proven act of sabotage in commercial aviation.

THE SINKING OF THE EDMUND FITZGERALD

Arguably the most well known Great Lakes shipwreck is the *Edmund Fitzgerald*. Newspaper headlines screamed of the loss of the ship. Radio and television spread the news around the world and Gordon Lightfoot immortalized the loss of the ship.

Most people first learned of the steamer *Edmund Fitzgerald* on November 10, 1975, the day the ship went missing, but to those who love the Great Lakes and freighters, the *Edmund Fitzgerald* was one of the most famous ships on the lakes.

On June 7, 1958, Mrs. Elizabeth Fitzgerald, wife of the ship's namesake smashed a bottle of champagne on the port bow of hull # 301 and said:

"I christen thee Edmund Fitzgerald. *God bless you."*

The giant ship slid sideways into a yard basin to the blasting of horns and whistles from more that 250 commercial and recreational vessels and the cheers of the over 15,000 well wishers gathered to witness the historic event.

Launched at the Great Lakes Engineering Works yard in River Rouge, Michigan, the *Fitzgerald* was the largest ship to sail the Great Lakes. The *Fitzgerald* measured 729 feet in length, the length of almost 2 ½ football

The Edmund Fitzgerald *passing through the St. Clair River.* From the Great Lakes photographic collection of Hugh Clark.

fields and 75 feet across. The *Fitzgerald* carried the longest ship distinction for 13 years when the 858 foot Roger Blough was launched.

The "Big Fitz", as she was affectionately called, was owned by the Northwestern Mutual Life Insurance Corporation of Milwaukee, Wisconsin, and joined the growing number of Great Lakes ships in the Northwestern fleet.

The fleet consisted of ships *J. Burton Ayers, Joseph S. Wood, and the J.H. Hillman Jr.* The Northwestern Mutual Life Insurance Corporation was in the business of investing in Great Lakes commerce not operating the ships, so the ship *Edmund Fitzgerald* was leased to the Columbia Transportation Division of Oglebay Norton Company of Cleveland, Ohio.

The *Edmund Fitzgerald* was named in honor of the newly elected Chairman of the Board of the Northwestern Mutual Life Insurance Corporation, Edmund Fitzgerald.

Mr. Fitzgerald distinguished himself by serving the company for over twenty-five years as a Vice President, President and Chairman of the Board. But, Fitzgerald is also a well-respected name in Great Lakes maritime history.

Mr. Fitzgerald's father, William Fitzgerald, was the president of the Milwaukee Dry Dock Company which later became known as the American Ship Building Company and William's father John and five of his brothers were all captains of Great Lakes sailing vessels.

In Gordon Lightfoot's ballad: *"The Wreck of the Edmund Fitzgerald"* a verse begins:

"The ship is the pride of the American Side..."

The *Edmund Fitzgerald* truly was the pride of the American side of the Great Lakes for she was the largest ship on the lakes. The *"Fitz,"* one of the many nick names she was affectionately called, carried the largest cargo of any the Great Lakes freighter and she could carry that cargo at a faster speed, about 16 MPH, than any other freighter as well.

In addition to her speed and cargo handling capabilities, the ship was also distinguished by her accommodations. They were unsurpassed by any Great Lakes freighter. In the uppermost forward deckhouse, the Texas Deck, was the chart room and the pilot house complete with the newest state of the art electronic communication and navigational equipment. Below on the foc'sle deck was the captain's office, stateroom and private bathroom.

Also on the foc'sle deck were two guest staterooms, lavishly furnished by Detroit's J. L. Hudson Company. The guest staterooms were reserved for executives and guests of Oglebay and Norton and the Northwestern Mutual Life Insurance Corporation. There was a large lounge facing aft

THE SINKING OF THE EDMUND FITZGERALD

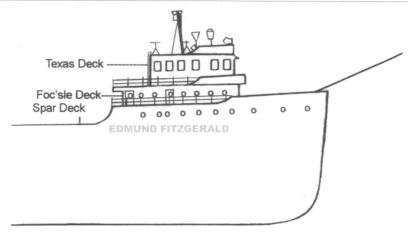

overlooking the cargo hatches of the ship with a pantry stocked full of drinks and snacks, for the pleasure of the guests .

Below the foc'sle deck is the weather or spar deck. On this level, in the forward deckhouse, are found the quarters for the 1st, 2nd, and 3rd Mates. Each had a private room with bathroom. Any unlicensed crew who worked in the pilothouse bunked two to a room on this deck.

Behind the forward deckhouse on the spar deck is the area of a Great Lakes freighter where the cargo hatches are located. On the *Edmund Fitzgerald* there were 21 cargo hatches.

Below the spar deck of the *Edmund Fitzgerald* is a cargo hold of 860,950 cubic feet. This area is divided into three non-water tight areas separated by screened bulkheads. Below the cargo hold and along both sides are the ballast tanks. The ballast tanks took on water for weight to control the ship's trim and to provide weight when the ship was traveling without cargo.

The after deckhouse is located above the engine room and contains the crew quarters, a TV room, card room, pool room, the galley and the mess (dining room) and two other dining rooms, one for the officers and the other for guests. Also on this deck, the Chief Engineer maintained an office and a private stateroom. In addition the 1st, 2nd and 3rd assistant engineers had private rooms. The crew quarters were large as crew accommodations go on Great Lake freighters. All of the non-licensed crew staterooms, each with a private bathroom, were air-conditioned and accommodated only two men.

The crew accommodations made the *Edmund Fitzgerald* one of the most sought after assignments on the lakes.

Travel between the after deckhouse and the forward deckhouse was accomplished on the open spar deck in fair weather. In times of high wind

GREAT LAKES DISASTERS

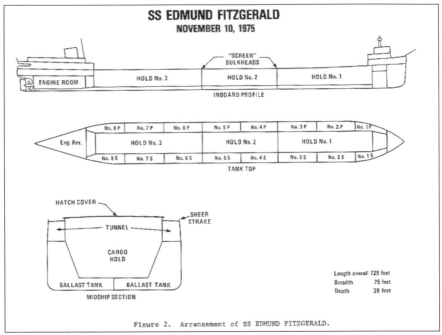

SS EDMUND FITZGERALD
NOVEMBER 10, 1975

Figure 2.   Arrangement of SS EDMUND FITZGERALD.

These drawings of the Edmund Fitzgerald, *from the Coast Guard Marine Causality Report, illustrates the location of the three cargo holds, the ballast tanks and the crew passage tunnels below the spar deck.*

or rough seas which could wash a crewmember overboard, travel between the two deckhouses was through two under deck passages or tunnels, which offered protection from the elements.

The 21 cargo hatches of the *Edmund Fitzgerald* had vertical steel walls, or combing, which rose 24 inches above the spar deck. The hatches were covered by 11 x 54 feet long hatch covers, made of a single piece of 5/16 inch thick hardened steel. The hatch covers were then held in place by 68 manually tightened Kestner Clamps. To reduce the amount of water that could enter the cargo hold in high seas a gasket around the perimeter of the hatch cover where it met the hatch combing was compressed as the clamps were tightened.

The cargo hatches were lifted or replaced with the use of an electrically operated hatch crane. The hatch crane traveled fore and aft on rails in the deck. The crane would be positioned over and made fast to a hatch cover. The operator would activate the crane to raise the heavy hatch cover. The crane would then roll out of the way for loading or unloading of cargo from that hatch.

THE SINKING OF THE EDMUND FITZGERALD

Once the operation was done the cargo hatches were replaced and secured down by a crew member manually tightening the Kestner Clamps.

In 1958, when the *Edmund Fitzgerald* was launched, the ship was not only the largest ship on the lakes but also the fastest. The ship impressed all with its speed of 16 MPH.

After her sea trials, on September 23, 1958, Captain Lambert, the *Edmund Fitzgerald's* first master, took the ship on her maiden voyage from its River Rouge berth up the Detroit River, through Lake St. Clair and the St. Clair River into the open water of Lake Huron. At Sault Ste. Marie the ship squeezed into the locks with much fanfare, clearing the lock gates with only inches on either side, then sailed into the clear blue waters of Lake Superior.

When the *"Big Fitz"* returned, she carried a load of taconite pellets which set a record for the largest cargo, by weight, to pass through the Soo Locks, the first of many records the ship would earn throughout her career.

Throughout the 1958 season the *"Mighty Fitz"* only called on two ports, Silver Bay, Minnesota, and Toledo, Ohio. These were the only two Great Lake ports that were large enough to accommodate a ship the size of the *Edmund Fitzgerald*.

During her last trip of the 1958 season, the *Fitzgerald* took on a load of taconite pellets in Minnesota and set out into Lake Superior. Captain Lambert was told that weather was building in the Plains States and that it would strike the Great Lakes with vengeance.

The Carl D. Bradley *lost on Lake Michigan on November 17, 1958. From the collection on the Bayliss Public Library, Sault Ste. Marie, Michigan.*

GREAT LAKES DISASTERS

As the *"Mighty Fitz"* crossed Lake Superior the weather held and the ship made good time, but shortly after entering northern Lake Huron the ship was assaulted by 80 mile per hour winds and waves up to 25 feet high. The *Edmund Fitzgerald* was severely battered by the wind and seas causing even veteran sailors to hunker down and question their chosen vocation.

It wasn't until the ship reached port in Toledo that the crew was informed of the sinking of *Carl D. Bradley* in upper Lake Michigan. The *Bradley's* crew, friends and associates of the men of the *Fitzgerald's* crew, were killed when the *Bradley* broke in two in the same storm that they had just sailed through.

For thirteen years the *Edmund Fitzgerald* held the distinction of being the largest ship on the Great Lakes. During that period the ship set several records for the amount of cargo carried including, in 1964, becoming the first ship to carry one million tons of cargo through the Soo Locks in a single season.

In testament to her designers and engineers the *Edmund Fitzgerald* remained virtually unchanged during her career. Any changes made were to improve on her performance with technology that was not available at the time of her launch. In 1969, a Byrd-Johnson diesel bow thruster was installed to better control the ship when entering and leaving the Soo Locks and to assist in docking.

The next improvement was the conversion of the main power plant from coal to oil. All of the equipment associated with the coal operation was removed and the new oil fired unit installed and fuel tanks were constructed in the old coal bunkers.

On November 9, 1975, the *Edmund Fitzgerald,* with Captain Ernest McSorley in command, lay moored at the Burlington Northern Railroad Dock # 1 east in Superior, Wisconsin. The *"Fitz"* took on 50,013 gallons of fuel from a fuel barge which tied up alongside as the ship took on its cargo of taconite pellets.

Taconite pellets are produced through a process by which taconite, a form of iron ore, is crushed into a fine powder. The powdered taconite is heated in rotating kilns to form reddish brown balls about one half inch in diameter.

The round pellets are easily transported on conveyer belts and railroad hopper cars that discharge from the bottom. The round shape of the pellets also packs more tightly in the cargo hold of a ship than raw irregular shaped iron ore, allowing the ship to carry more cargo.

The cargo loading facility at the Burlington Dock was equipped with storage bins or pockets built high above the deck of a ship. The taconite

THE SINKING OF THE EDMUND FITZGERALD

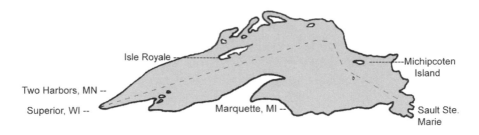

pellets were loaded into hopper cars that were pushed by a locomotive up on top of the dock and located over the pockets. Once in position, the bottom of the hopper car was opened and the pellets fell into the pockets.

To load a ship like the *Edmund Fitzgerald*, the ship would be moored along side the dock with its cargo hatches aligned with the loading chutes on the dock. The chutes would be lowered into the cargo hatches, a gate lifted and the taconite pellets would roll down into the hold of the ship.

The cargo was loaded into the ship under the direction of the Chief Mate. It was his responsibility to maintain the ship's trim and draft while loading. He directed the pumping out of ballast water while the cargo was loaded so the ship remained on an "even keel".

At approximately 7:30 AM on November 9, 1975, the *Edmund Fitzgerald* was moored starboard side to the dock. The pockets had been filled earlier and the procedure began.

The first chute to be lowered and discharged was into cargo hatch number 21, the hatch furthest aft. A load of approximately 300 tons poured into the hold of the *Fitzgerald*.

The ship was then shifted aft twelve feet so the next chute was aligned with hatch number 20.

This filling of taconite pellets, the pumping out of ballast water and the moving to align with the chutes continued until 1:15 PM. By then the *Fitzgerald* had taken on a cargo of 26, 116 tons to be delivered to the steel mill at Zug Island in the Detroit River.

Once loaded with the taconite pellets, the crew of the *Edmund Fitzgerald* readied the ship to depart from Superior, Wisconsin.

The trip would cover approximately 750 miles, taking the ship across the length of Lake Superior, through the locks at Sault Ste. Marie, down the St. Mary's River into northern Lake Huron, over 200 miles down the length of Lake Huron into the St. Clair River and Lake St. Clair finally to Zug Island on the Detroit River. For the *Edmund Fitzgerald*, it would be a 5 day trip.

GREAT LAKES DISASTERS

On November 9, 1975, at approximately 2:15 PM, the *"Mighty Fitz"* steamed away from the Burlington Docks in Superior, Wisconsin. The ship assumed the recommended course to transit Lake Superior.

After two hours the *Fitzgerald* was off Two Harbors, Minnesota, where the Great Lakes freighter *Arthur M. Anderson* of the United States Steel Corporation, was departing with a cargo of taconite pellets en route to Gary, Indiana.

The captain of the *Anderson*, Jesse Cooper, received a radio transmission from the National Weather Service announcing they had posted gale warnings for Lake Superior. Sighting a ship several miles to the southwest of his position, Captain Cooper radioed the ship.

> Cooper: *"W4805,* Arthur M. Anderson *to the vessel northbound abeam Knife River. Do you read me?"*
>
> McSorley*:* "Anderson, *this is the* Edmund Fitzgerald. *Over"*
>
> Cooper: *"This is the* Anderson. *Have you picked up the gale warnings the Weather Service just posted? Over."*
>
> McSorley: *"This is the* Fitzgerald, *ah, roger."*
>
> Cooper: *"I'm thinking I will take the northern track; get over to the north shore for shelter in case it really starts to blow. Over."*
>
> McSorley: *"I've been thinking the same thing. I'm steering sixty-five degrees for Isle Royale."*

Captains Cooper and McSorley elected to abandon the more direct southern course across the lake for a course which would take them more towards the northern shore of Lake Superior. It was not uncommon for lake vessels to use the northern route and let the Canadian landmass provide shelter. The two ships agreed to travel the same course.

On November 8, a meteorological disturbance developed over the Oklahoma Panhandle. At that time it was expected to become a typical fall storm and pass south of Lake Superior. But by 9:00 am on November 9, a new prediction had the storm crossing the eastern end of Lake Superior on up into Canada.

Ten hours later, at 7:00 pm, the National Weather Service issued a gale warning for the lake, meaning winds from 40 to 52 miles per hour were expected.

THE SINKING OF THE EDMUND FITZGERALD

The Arthur M. Anderson. *From the collection on the Port Huron Museum.*

Some Great Lake ships are local weather reporters. They call in at 1:00 am, 7:00 am, 1:00 pm and 7:00 pm to give their position and relate the weather at their location. Both the *Anderson* and *Fitzgerald* participated in this program.

The *Edmund Fitzgerald* provided a weather report on November 10 at 1:00 in the morning. She reported the winds at 60 miles per hour from the north northeast and the waves were running at 10 feet. Their location at the time was 20 miles south of Isle Royale.

An hour later the National Weather Service issued a storm warning with expected winds in excess of 60 miles per hour and up to 15-foot seas. The captains of both ships knew they would be in for a long night on Lake Superior.

The faster *Fitzgerald* passed the *Anderson* as the two ships made their way through the horrendous conditions. On shore a 60-mile per hour wind could uproot trees, and do structural damage to buildings. On a ship in the middle of Lake Superior, the winds would easily blow a man overboard and anything not securely bolted down would be ripped from the ship.

GREAT LAKES DISASTERS

The wind was horrible but the huge wind whipped waves crashed on the ships covering their deck with cascading torrents of water with enough force to wash anything overboard.

At 7:00 am on November 10, the *Edmund Fitzgerald* reported its position as 35 miles north of Copper Harbor, Michigan on the tip of the Keweenaw Peninsula. Ten-foot waves were pounding the ship and 40 + mile per hour winds blasted the ship.

Five hours later, the ships had traveled about 60 miles since the last report, the *Anderson* radioed in a weather report. The winds were from the southeast at approximately 23 miles per hour with waves at 12 feet. Their position was 20 miles northwest of Michipicoten Island. The *Fitzgerald* did not issue a weather report, but the *Anderson* had the *Fitzgerald* position as 11 miles northwest of the island.

Captains Cooper and McSorley communicated about the course they would follow along the Canadian shore southeast towards the locks at Sault Ste. Marie. The master of the *Anderson* elected to head west a ways to pass clear of Michipicoten Island. Captain McSorley responds:

McSorley: *"Well, I am rolling some, but I think I'll hold the course until I'm ready to turn for Caribou."*

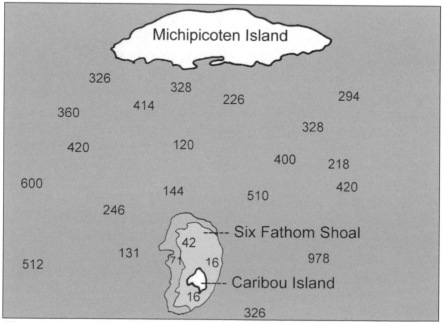

The shallow Six Fathom Shoal surrounds Caribou Island. The numbers in the drawing represent depths in feet.

THE SINKING OF THE EDMUND FITZGERALD

At 3:15 pm, the *Edmund Fitzgerald* changed its course to pass between Caribou Island and Michipicoten Island. On the bridge of the *Arthur Anderson* Captain Copper watched the *Fitzgerald's* course on the radar. He called first mate, Morgan Clark, to take a look. They discussed how close the *Fitzgerald* was to Six Fathom Shoal. Captain Cooper remarked they are in closer than he would want his ship to be.

The Six Fathom Shoal is a shallow rocky shoal surrounding Caribou Island. The island, approximately 3.5 miles north to south and less than 1.5 miles across, is located 21 miles south of Michipicoten Island. Between the islands the water is several hundred feet deep but the shoal surrounding the island has depths from 42 to 16 feet.

About 3:30 pm Captain McSorley called Captain Cooper.

McSorley: *"Anderson this is the Fitzgerald. I have sustained some topside damage. I have a fence rail laid down, two vents lost or damaged, and a list. I'm checking down. Will you stay by me till I get to Whitefish?"*

Cooper: *"Charlie on that Fitzgerald. Do you have your pumps going?"*

McSorley: *"Yes, both of them."*

By checking down, Captain McSorley meant he was going to reduce the *Fitzgerald's* speed so the *Anderson* could catch up with them. At that time the *Fitzgerald* was about 15 miles ahead of the *Anderson*. The ships were heading for Whitefish Bay on the southeast shore of Lake Superior. There they could anchor in the bay and wait out better weather to continue on to the Soo Locks.

The *Edmund Fitzgerald* was fitted with several vents so it's not known which of them Captain McSorley was speaking of. The port and starboard access tunnels had vents fore and aft and each ballast tank was equipped with a vent. If the vents were damaged or lost, lake water would pour in through the openings to be removed by the pumps.

The ship was equipped with four 7,000 gallon per minute ballast pumps and two 2,000 gallon per minute auxiliary pumps.

Forty minutes later, Captain McSorley contacted the Anderson by radio.

McSorley: *"Anderson, this is the Fitzgerald. I have lost both radars. Can you provide me with radar plots till we reach Whitefish Bay?"*

Cooper: *"Charlie on that,* Fitzgerald. *We'll keep you advised of your position."*

The *Edmund Fitzgerald* was heading southeast in the storm tossed waters of Lake Superior. The ship had sustained damage and had a list to starboard. The wind, grown to hurricane force intensity, beat down on her and waves as high as a two and half story building were mounting the ship from her stern and washing over her decks. Now both radars are inoperable.

The radar didn't work but the *Fitzgerald* was equipped with a radio directional finder (RDF). An RDF is an electronic device that determines the direction a radio signal is coming from. The Coast Guard maintained stations around the Great Lakes to transmit radio signals for ships to pick up and plot their position. The *Fitzgerald* was trying to pick up the signal from Whitefish Point so they could set a course to Whitefish Bay.

Unable to pick up the signal from Whitefish Point, Captain McSorley radioed the Coast Guard at Grand Marais to check if the radio beacon was functional. Both the Whitefish Point radio beacon and the lighthouse had been knocked out by the storm.

The *Edmund Fitzgerald* had no radar and it couldn't pick up the Whitefish Point radio beacon so the ship was traveling blind. The *Fitzgerald* had to depend on the *Anderson* to guide it to the safety of Whitefish Bay.

Between 5:30 and 6:00 pm, Captain Cedric, a Great Lakes Pilot aboard the Swedish ship *Avafors*, established radio communication with the *Fitzgerald*.

Cedric: "Fitzgerald, *this is the* Avafors. *I have the Whitefish light now but still am receiving no beacon. Over."*

McSorley: *"I'm very glad to hear it."*

Cedric: *"The wind is really howling down here. What are the conditions where you are?"*

Captain Cedric overhears Captain McSorley shouting at someone on the *Fitzgerald*:

McSorley: *"Don't let nobody on deck! (unintelligible)* "... vents"

Cedric: *"What's that,* Fitzgerald? *Unclear. Over."*

McSorley*: "I have a bad list, lost both radars. And am taking heavy seas over the deck. One of the worst seas I've ever been in."*

THE SINKING OF THE EDMUND FITZGERALD

Cedric: *"If I'm correct, you have two radars."*

McSorley: *"They're both gone."*

The *Anderson* was buffeted by the horrifying winds, gusting in excess of 100 miles per hour, blinding snow squalls and tremendous waves, running 16 to 26 feet, as it traveled towards the protection Whitefish Bay offered. It was making up time on the *Fitzgerald* that was now only 10 miles ahead of her position.

Captain Jesse Cooper reported sometime before 7:00 pm the *Anderson* was assaulted by two immense waves. The waves covered the ship's spar deck with green water to a depth of 12 feet, making the wave, he estimated, over 35 feet in height!

The wave crashed down on the stern of the *Anderson* with such force that the aft lifeboat, sitting on a saddle, was forced down, leaving an impression of the saddle in the metal of the lifeboat.

The two waves far exceeded the average waves on the lake for that time period. A wave or waves higher than the predominate waves are not uncommon on the lakes. Called a rogue wave, they travel along the surface of the lake combining with other waves, absorbing their energy and mounting in height.

First mate Clark, on the *Anderson*, sighted a north bound ship on the radar ahead of the *Fitzgerald* and radioed them at 7:10 pm to relay the information.

Clark: "Fitzgerald, *this is the* Anderson. *Have you checked down?"*

McSorley: *"Yes, we have."*

The Arthur M. Anderson. *From the Hugh Clark Great Lakes Photographic collection.*

Clark: Fitzgerald, *we are about 10 miles behind you, and gaining about 1 ½ miles per hour.* Fitzgerald, *there is a target 19 miles ahead of us. So the target would be 9 miles on ahead of you."*

McSorley: *"Well, am I going to clear?"*

Clark: *"Yes. He is going to pass to the west of you."*

McSorley: *"Well, fine."*

Clark: *"By the way,* Fitzgerald, *how are you making out with your problems?"*

McSorley: *"We are holding our own."*

Clark: *"Okay, fine. I'll be talking to you later."*

At times the lights of the *Fitzgerald* could be seen from the *Anderson* in the distance. But shortly after the transmission, the lights of the *Fitzgerald* were obscured by a snow squall.

Ten minutes later the squall cleared. The men on the bridge of the *Anderson* could see the lights of three up-bound vessels but not the lights of the *Fitzgerald*.

Captain Cooper checked the *Anderson's* radar. There was no sign of the *Fitzgerald*. Moments later a target was seen on the radar but it disappeared.

The *Anderson* attempted to call the *Fitzgerald* on the radio. There wasn't an answer. He called a "saltie" in the area, still no reply. Could the storm have blown out the *Anderson's* radio, and it wasn't transmitting? To check Captain Cooper called the steamer *William Clay Ford*. They received the call and responded. The radio worked, it's the *Fitzgerald* that wasn't receiving or transmitting.

At 7:39 pm, the Anderson called the Sault Ste. Marie Coast Guard to report they could not locate the *Fitzgerald* visually, by radar or by radio.

They again contacted the Coast Guard at 7:55 pm to inform them that they had lost communication and sight of the *Fitzgerald*.

At 8:32 pm Captain Cooper again called the Coast Guard;

Cooper: " *Soo Control, this is the* Anderson. *I am very concerned about the welfare of the steamer* Edmund Fitzgerald. *He was right in front of us, experiencing a little difficulty. He was taking on a small amount of water and none of the upbound ships have passed him. I can see no lights as before and I don't have him on radar. I just hope he didn't take a nose dive!"*

Soo Control: *"This is Soo Control. Roger. Thank you for the information. We will try and contact him. Over."*

At 9:00 pm Coast Guard Group Soo called the *Arthur Anderson*;

Group Soo: *"Anderson, this is Group Soo. What is your position?"*

Captain Cooper: *"We're down here, about two miles off Parisienne Island right now ...the wind is northwest forty to forty-five miles here in the bay."*

Group Soo: *"Is it calming down at all, do you think?"*

Captain Cooper: *"In the bay it is, but I heard a couple of salties talking up there, and they wish they hadn't gone out."*

Group Soo: *"Do you think there is any possibility that you could ...ah ...come about and go back there and do any searching?"*

Coast Guard Station Sault Ste. Marie did not have a vessel available that could go out in the lake with the wind and wave conditions on Lake Superior.

Captain Cooper: *"Ah... God, I don't know... that... that sea out there is tremendously large. Ah ...if you want me to, I can, but I'm not going to be making any time: I'll be lucky to make two or three miles an hour going back out that way."*

The *Anderson* had just gone through hell to get to the safety of Whitefish Bay, and now Captain Cooper was asked to put his ship and crew in jeopardy to go back out into the howling wind and 16 to 35 foot seas to look for the *Edmund Fitzgerald* or possibly her crew in lifeboats or life rafts.

Group Soo: *"Well, you'll have to make a decision whether you will be hazarding your vessel or not, but you're probably one of the only vessels right now that can get to the scene. We're going to try to contact those saltwater vessels and see if they can't possibly come back also...*

things look pretty bad right now: it looks like she may have split apart at the seams like the Morrell *did a few years back."*

All three of the saltwater vessels told the Coast Guard that they didn't think they could come about due to the severity of the conditions.

Captain Cooper: *"Well, that's what I been thinking. But we were talking to him about seven and he said that everything was going fine. He said that he was going along like an old shoe; no problems at all."*

Group Soo: *"Well, again do you think you could come about and go back and have a look in the area?"*

Captain Cooper: *"Well, I'll go back and take a look, but, God, I'm afraid I'm going to take a hell of a beating out there…I'll turn around and give it a whirl, but God, I don't know. I'll give it a try."*

Group Soo: *"That would be good…"*

Captain Cooper: *"You do realize what the conditions are out there?"*

There isn't an immediate response from Coast Guard Group Soo.

Captain Cooper: *"You do realize what the conditions are out there, don't you?*

Group Soo: *"Affirmative. From what your reports are I can appreciate the conditions. Again, though, I have to leave that decision up to you as to whether it would be haz-arding your vessel or not. If you think you can safely go back up to that area, I would request that you do so. But, I have to leave the decision up to you."*

Captain Cooper: *"I'll give it a try, but that's all I can do."*

The Coast Guard Air Station at Traverse City had a fixed wing HU-16 aircraft in the air within 30 minutes, while the Group Soo 110 foot harbor tug, *Naugatuck*, went to Whitefish Bay but was ordered not to go into the lake. Coast Guard regulations prohibited the *Naugatuck* from operating in conditions when winds are in excess of 60 miles per hour.

THE SINKING OF THE EDMUND FITZGERALD

The Hilda Marjanne. *From the Hugh Clark Great Lakes Photographic collection.*

There were other ships at anchor in the safety of Whitefish Bay; the *William Clay Ford, Hilda Marjanne, William R. Roesch, Benjamin F. Fairless, Frontenac, Murray Bay* and *Algosoo.* The Coast Guard requested them to go back into the lake and search for the missing *Fitzgerald* or survivors of her crew. Only the 629 foot *William Clay Ford* and the 504 foot *Hilda Marjanne* agreed to venture out into the tempest and search for their fellow sailors.

The wind was blowing in excess of 50 miles per hour with gusts much higher, as the ships plowed into the huge waves slowly making their way towards the last known position of the *Fitzgerald.* After a short time the captain of the smaller *Hilda Marjanne* determined the conditions were too much for his vessel and had to return to Whitefish Bay.

The *William Clay Ford* and the *Arthur M. Anderson* searched throughout the night. As the conditions dissipated, the two ships were joined by the *Armco, Roger Blough, Reserve, Wilfred Sykes, William R. Roesch, Frontenac, John O. McKellar* and the *Murray Bay.*

Aiding in the search from the air were a C-130 from the Air National Guard, a Canadian Coast Guard C-130, and three helicopters from the Coast Guard Air Station at Traverse City, Michigan.

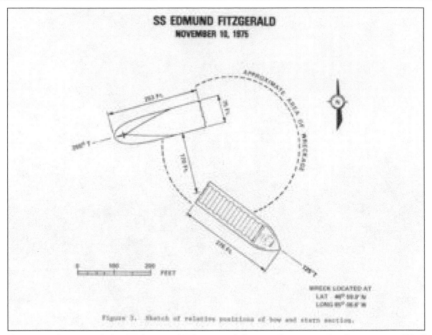

The wreckage of the Edmund Fitzgerald *as it lies on the bottom of Lake Superior*. From the Coast Guard Marine Causality Report.

The ships and aircraft searched the eastern end of Lake Superior throughout the night and for the next few days. All that was found from the *Edmund Fitzgerald* was a lifeboat, half of another, two inflatable life rafts, twenty-one life jackets or pieces of them, and other pieces of flotsam. No ship, no survivors, no bodies were found.

On November 16, 1975, two large objects lying close to one another were found on the bottom of Lake Superior. Successive sonar searches and photographs taken by an unmanned remotely operated submarine verified the targets on the bottom were indeed the *Edmund Fitzgerald*.

The *Fitzgerald* lays in approximately 530 feet of water, at a position of 46.59.9 N, 85.06.6 W. just in Canadian water, seventeen miles northwest from the safety of Whitefish Point.

The 729 foot ship was broken in two parts; a 276 foot bow section in an upright position with the stern section lying upside-down at an angle to the bow section. An approximately 200 foot long mid section was reduced to pieces and lies within the wreck site.

In the weeks, months and years that followed the sinking, the *Edmund Fitzgerald* was the subject of investigations by many organizations

THE SINKING OF THE EDMUND FITZGERALD

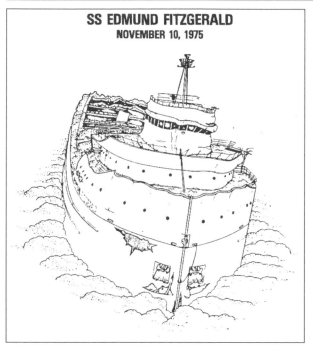

SS EDMUND FITZGERALD
NOVEMBER 10, 1975

The bow section of the Edmund Fitzgerald. *From the Coast Guard Marine Causality Report.*

including the Coast Guard Marine Board of Investigation, The National Transportation Safety Board and the Lakes Carriers' Association.

Theories of what caused the *Edmund Fitzgerald* to sink are plentiful and range from the plausible to the absurd. But they are all just theories. There is not a definitive answer, as of yet, as to the cause of the loss.

The Coast Guard Marine Board came to the conclusion that the cause of the

The stern section of the Edmund Fitzgerald. *From the Coast Guard Marine Causality Report.*

sinking of the *Edmund Fitzgerald* was possibly due to massive flooding of the cargo hold. They based this on their observation of undamaged cargo hold clamps.

The Coast Guard underwater photographs revealed some of the hatch clamps to be bent and distorted from the stress of the hatch covers being ripped off during the ship's plunge and impact with the bottom of the lake. Yet many hatch clamps were un-damaged, leading to the conclusion of the Coast Guard that many of the hatch clamps were not properly adjusted and worked loose or were not latched down in the first place. They based this assumption on the proposition that if the clamps were properly tightened down before the ship sunk they should be distorted after the accident.

If the hatch clamps were not in place or improperly adjusted, lake water could gain access to the cargo hold. Since the three cargo holds were separated by a screen rather than watertight bulkheads, the water could migrate throughout the ship.

This theory is based on evidence shown on the photographs but many first hand reports from men who had sailed on the *Fitzgerald* said that Captain McSorley would never had permitted the *Fitzgerald* to leave port without the hatch covers being properly secured. They said that some of the clamps were damaged and did not work but there were more than enough that did function correctly.

Another widely accepted theory of the cause of the sinking of the *Fitzgerald*, one that the Lake Carriers' Association supports, is that the ship struck bottom and was damaged while crossing Six Fathom Shoal.

Captain Cooper of the *Arthur Anderson* testified that he observed the *Fitzgerald* on the radar and he stated to his mate that the ship was closer to Six Fathom Shoal than he would want his ship to be.

While the lake is several hundred feet deep between Michipicoten and Caribou Islands, the shallow rocky reef surrounding Caribou extends almost five miles to the north with depths less than 40 feet. A ship in waves of 16 to 25 feet or greater could easily scrape the bottom in shallow water while the ship was in the trough of the waves.

It is possible that the *Fitzgerald* came too close to the shoal, grounded causing bottom plates to rupture and allowing water to enter the ballast tanks. Possibly Captain McSorley thought the water in the ballast tanks was coming from the missing vents when actually it was from the vents and from the damaged bottom. The pumps could not remove the water fast enough and the ship would take on a list and eventually lose its buoyancy and sink.

THE SINKING OF THE EDMUND FITZGERALD

While this is a valid theory the upside-down stern section does not show any evidence, scratches or punctures, of it scrapping along the rocky shoal and subsequent dives on the Six Fathom Shoal did not show any recent scrapes.

Captain Cooper told of two approximately 35-foot waves that were much larger than the storm's predominate waves. He holds to the theory that the two rogue waves hit the *Fitzgerald* on the stern and covered the entire spar deck with several feet of water. This water raced forward along the spar deck of the ship crashing to a stop and mounting at the foreword deckhouse. The extra weight of the water so far forward on the ship forced the bow down and the ship could not recover quickly enough to rise with the next wave. Instead the *Edmund Fitzgerald* dove below the surface of Lake Superior until it struck and broke up on the bottom.

Some people theorize that the *Edmund Fitzgerald* broke apart on the surface before she dove to the bottom. They point to the fact that in a storm with large waves, a ship the length of the *Fitzgerald* might have been subjected to stress fractures in her hull.

The fractures could have occurred as the hull flexed while riding the huge waves. A 729 foot ship such as the *Fitzgerald* is not fully supported along its entire length in large waves, rather a wave might be under the foreword section of the ship and the next wave might be towards the stern leaving the center unsupported. Possibly the next wave might support the center while the bow and stern sections are unsupported. This flexing of the hull could result in stress fractures that could lead the ship to break apart.

Whatever happened on that night of November 10, 1975, it occurred quickly, the ship never had time to radio a distress call.

A definitive cause of the sinking of the 729-foot *Edmund Fitzgerald* has not yet been discovered and it might never be. There are not any eye witnesses who can tell of the last few hours and minutes of the ship's existence. Most of what is known is from the radio transmissions between the *Fitzgerald* and the *Anderson* and other ships, but the communications are void of details. The remains of the ship provides some clues but there are still more questions than answers.

What is known for sure is that the *Edmund Fitzgerald* departed Superior, Wisconsin with a load of 26,116 tons of iron ore pellets, a crew of 29 men and the ship never arrived. The wreckage of the ship has been found but the men are still listed as missing.

GREAT LAKES DISASTERS

The Edmund Fitzgerald. *From the collections of the Port Huron Museum.*

**In Honor of the
Crew of the**
Edmund Fitzgerald

Ernest M. McSorley,	63	Captain	Toledo Ohio
John H. McCarthy,	62	Mate	Bay Village, Ohio
James A. Pratt,	44,	sec. mate	Lakewood, Ohio
Michael E. Armagost,	37	third mate	Iron River, Wisconsin
Thomas Bentsen,	23	oiler	St. Joseph, Michigan
Thomas D. Borgeson,	41	maint. man	Duluth, Minnesota
John D. Simmons,	60	wheelsman	Ashland, Wisconsin
Eugene W. O'Brien,	50	wheelsman	St. Paul, Minnesota
John J. Poviach,	59	wheelsman	Bradenton, Florida
Ranson E. Cundy,	53	watchman	Superior, Wisconsin
William J. Spengler,	59	watchman	Toledo, Ohio
Karl A. Peckol,	20	watchman	Ashtabula, Ohio
Mark A. Thomas,	21	deck hand	Richmond Heights, Ohio
Paul M. Riippa,	22	deck hand	Ashtabula, Ohio
Bruce L. Hudson,	22	deck hand	North Olmsted, Ohio
David E. Weiss,	22	cadet	Agoura, California

THE SINKING OF THE EDMUND FITZGERALD

Robert C. Rafferty,	62	steward	Toledo, Ohio
Allen G. Kalmon,	43	sec. cook	Washburn, Wisconsin
Frederick J. Beetcher,	56	porter	Superior, Wisconsin
Nolan F. Church,	55	porter	Silver Bay, Minnesota
George J. Holl,	60	chief eng.	Cabot, Pennsylvania
Edward F. Bindon,	47	1st asst. eng.	Fairport Harbor, Ohio
Thomas E. Edwards,	50	2nd asst. eng.	Oregon, Ohio
Russell G. Haskell,	40	3rd asst. eng.	Millbury, Ohio
Oliver J. Champeau,	41	3rd asst. eng.	Milwaukee, Wisconsin
Blaine H. Wilhelm,	52	oiler	Moquah, Wisconsin
Ralph G. Walton,	58	oiler	Fremont, Ohio
Joseph W. Mazes,	59	maintenance	Ashland, Wisconsin
Gordon F. MacLellan,	30	wiper	Clearwater, Florida

(Authors Note: For a complete and detailed history, career and sinking of the *Edmund Fitzgerald* it is recommended to read; "The Wreck of the *Edmund Fitzgerald*" by Frederick Stonehouse. Published by Avery Color Studios.)

FLIGHT 191 - CHICAGO TO LOS ANGELES

Two ladies studied the arrivals board at Los Angeles International Airport. They found American Airlines Flight 191 from Chicago but no arrival time was listed, only a statement that read; "See Agent". They went to the desk and were told there had been an accident.

A man ran into the airport and inquired at the American Airlines desk about Flight 191, he had just heard on the radio a Chicago to Los Angeles bound airplane had crashed. He was told it was the plane his brother was on.

In the Chicago suburb of Wilmette, neighbors of the Sutton family: Steve, Caroline and their two sons, Colin 9 and Chris age 7, were grieving for they would never see the family again. The Sutton family was on Flight 191 bound to Los Angeles to meet Caroline's parents and brother. The boys had been excited and they had told everyone they were going to Disneyland.

On May 25, 1979, American Airlines Flight 191 crashed on take off killing 273 people; making it the worst accident in the history of United States commercial aviation.

American Airlines Flight 191 was a McDonnell Douglas DC-10. The DC-10 was one of the three "Jumbo" jets flying in North America at the time. The other two were the Lockheed L-1011, and Boeing's 747.

The DC-10 was indeed a jumbo jet with an overall length of 181 feet and a wingspan over 155 feet, a passenger capacity of 255 to 270 plus crew, and the fuselage was almost twenty feet wide. Seating in the DC-10 cabin was nine seats across; two on the side, an aisle, five seats in the center, another aisle then two more seats.

The DC-10's military configuration, the KC-10 extender. From the United States Air Force.

American Airlines was first to introduce the DC-10 in 1971. McDonnell Douglas manufactured 386 of the mid to long range airliner until production was discontinued in 1988. The Air Force purchased sixty of the aircraft that they had reconfigured for air-to-air refueling.

The widebody jetliner had three General Electric CF-6-6D engines, two mounted on pylons beneath the wings and one on the tail or vertical stabilizer. The engines pushed the DC-10 along at a maximum cruising speed of 610 miles per hour.

The DC-10 was one of the most technologically advanced aircraft of its time but despite its innovations, the aircraft had a history of problems. Structural problems were blamed for several incidents.

In 1972, an American Airlines DC-10 flying out of Detroit's Metropolitan Airport suffered a catastrophic decompression in the main cabin and cargo bay. The rear cabin door had blown off while the aircraft was over Windsor, Ontario.

With rapid decompression of the cabin and cargo bay, the cabin floor crumpled under the enormous pressure. All three of the airplane's flight control systems are under the floor and were ruptured. Fortunately the pilot was able to fly the aircraft back to the airport by thrusting the engines to steer the aircraft.

Another door failure occurred on a Turkish Airlines McDonnell Douglas DC-10. Five minutes after the airplane took off from a Paris, France airport, on March 3, 1974, the aircraft smashed into the ground killing everyone aboard.

A cargo door had been compromised causing sudden depression of the cargo bay. The cabin floor became distorted from the decompression and severed the hydraulics governing the flight control systems rendering the aircraft uncontrollable.

An artist's conception of the Turkish Airlines DC-10 air disaster outside Paris, France. Drawing courtesy of the Wikipedia Commons photographic collection.

FLIGHT 191 - CHICAGO TO LOS ANGELES

Wreckage field from the crash of American Airlines Flight 191. From the National Transportation Safety.

The Turkish Airlines DC-10 had been reconfigured for maximum seating capacity and carried 346 passengers and crew, making it the worst single airplane air disaster in the history of aviation.

The McDonnell Douglas DC-10 jumbo jet had also experienced difficulties with its engines. In 1972, a Continental Airlines Los Angeles to Chicago flight took off and one of its engines malfunctioned and sections of the engine fell to the runway. The pilot was able to complete rotation (liftoff) with the two remaining engines and returned to the airport without any injuries to the passengers or crew.

The tail-mounted engine on a United Airlines DC-10 blew up in flight after taking off from O'Hare Airport in 1978. Parts of the engine rained shrapnel on downtown Elmhurst, Illinois. The aircraft returned to the airport and landed safely.

On May 25, 1979, American Airlines Chicago to Los Angeles Flight 191 taxied towards runway 32R as the flight crew performed the pre-flight checklist. The passengers were receiving safety information from the ten flight attendants; Linda Bundens, Barbara Burns, James Dehart, Carmen Fowler, Catherine Hiebert, Carol Ohm, Linda Prince, Michael Schassburger, Nancy Sullivan, and Sally Jo Titterington.

The captain of Flight 191 was Walter Lux. The 53 year old captain had in excess of 22,000 in-flight hours and had been flying the DC-10 aircraft since their introduction eight years earlier. The first officer was James

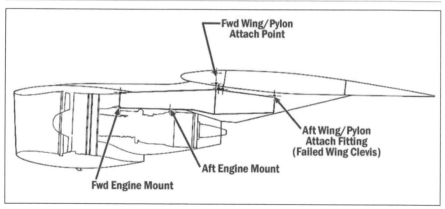

An illustration from the National Transportation Safety Board showing the failure point of the engine pylon.

Dillard, 49, and flight engineer was Alfred Udovich, 56, both experienced pilots with American Airlines.

After receiving clearance from the O'Hare flight control tower the widebody jet started its rollout down the runway. The Captain at the controls eased the throttles forward as first officer Dillard studied the instruments.

"V-1", the first officer announced as the aircraft had reached a speed too fast to abort the take off.

The first officer then reported, "V-R". Indicating the aircraft had attained the speed needed for rotation or to liftoff the runway.

Just seconds before or after liftoff the pylon holding the left engine to the underside of the wing broke free. Since the engine was in full thrust for takeoff, the engine propelled forward and up across the leading edge of the wing, tearing off a three-foot section of the leading edge of the wing.

The wings were set in an attitude for take off with slats down to create lift. When the engine fell from and thrust over the wing, it severed the hydraulic lines and the left wing slat retracted.

As Flight 191 rotated off runway 32 R, about 6,000 feet from brakes-off and climbed to approximately 325 feet, the right wing continued to create lift while the damaged left wing lost lift, causing the aircraft to roll to the left as it gained altitude.

The McDonnell Douglas DC-10 was designed to be able to achieve flight with the loss of one engine. But no aircraft can take off without the wings producing adequate lift to support the weight of the aircraft.

Chicago Tribune

Saturday, May 26, 1979

5 Star Final
★★★★★

6 Sections   15¢

Worst U.S. crash; 272 die at O'Hare

Flight 191 rolled until it was 112 degrees from horizontal, the nose dipped and the aircraft crashed into a field near the Oasis Mobile Home Court. The entire flight lasted 31 seconds.

The wreckage scattered to Oasis Mobile Home Court killing two residents, as well as everyone onboard Flight 191; thirteen American Airlines crew and 258 passengers. Two hundred and seventy three lives were lost.

The American Airlines jumbo jet burst into a huge ball of flames as the thousands of pounds of aviation fuel spewed from the ruptured wing tanks.

Investigators from the National Transportation Safety Board reported to the wreckage to determine the cause of the accident.

They knew the left engine had fallen from the aircraft but wanted to determine why it had fallen and how it contributed to the resulting destruction of the DC-10 and the death of all aboard.

The air safety investigators found the destruction and fire of the aircraft to be so devastating that little could be gleaned from it but the left engine was laying just off runway 32R.

The engines on a DC-10 were attached in two places to a pylon. The pylon then was attached to the wing at forward and aft locations.

After a forensic examination of the left engine, the investigators found the engine had not become detached from the pylon rather the pylon had detached from the wing. The aft wing/pylon attachment fitting had failed during take off, allowing the aft pylon to drop down and changed the thrust of the engine to a forward and upper direction. The engine powered up, then over the top of the wing tearing off part of the leading edge of the wing. The engine then fell to the runway.

The pilots did not know the full extent of the situation. From the cockpit of the DC-10, the pilots could not see the wings. They could tell

121

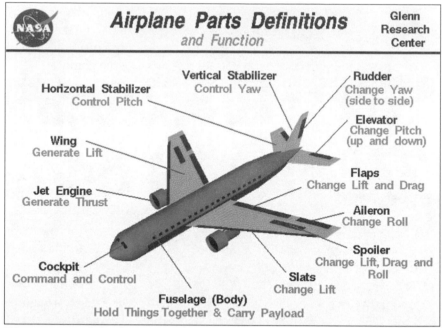

The parts and the function of a commercial jet airliner. The illustration is from the NASA collection.

the engine had dropped off but were unaware of the damage to the leading edge of the wing.

The aircraft was rolling to starboard yet there was no stall warning indicator and the instrument that would alert the pilots that the slats of wings were in disagreement was not functioning. The hydraulics operating the left wing was not functioning.

All that the pilots knew was the aircraft was rolling to the left but the cockpit instruments did not indicate it, and when they tried to compensate by adjusting the flaps and ailerons on the left wing, nothing happened because the hydraulics had been severed.

There was nothing the pilots could do to avert the accident once the port side (left) engine dropped off the wing. They had lost control of American Airlines Flight 191.

The National Transportation Safety Board had discovered that the lack of lift and the damage to the left wing had caused Flight 191 to go down but they needed to know why the aft pylon fitting had failed, allowing the engine to drop from the wing.

FLIGHT 191 - CHICAGO TO LOS ANGELES

The investigators had determined that the pylon had been damaged prior to the accident. When the engine had been removed eight weeks earlier for maintenance. American Airlines mechanics removed the engine and pylon assembly together with a forklift supporting the engine.

McDonnell Douglas recommends the engine be removed first then the pylon to reduce the risk of damage. However, American found they could remove both engine and pylon at one time and save over 200 hours of labor over the recommended method.

McDonnell Douglas recommended the two be removed separately, however they did not have the authority to insist it be done their way.

The crash of American Airlines Flight 191 was found to be the result of American Airlines maintenance procedures. The airline saved hundreds of hours of labor but 273 men, women and children were killed when Flight 191 crashed on take off on May 25, 1979.

Wreckage from the crash of American Airlines Flight 191. From the National Transportation Safety Board.

THE METROPOLITAN STORE EXPLOSION

Natural gas today is the primary source of fuel for most urban areas. It provides a flame for stoves and ovens, water heaters, and furnaces. It burns cleaner than wood, coal or oil and pumps less pollution into the atmosphere.

Natural gas is a bi-product of the oil industry. It is removed from oil during processing or it can be harvested at the oil well itself.

Early in the history of oil drilling, the natural gas was a nuisance. It had little or no commercial value and was burned off at the site. Developments in the industry found that the gas could be processed until it is almost all methane and pumped through pipelines to the customer.

Today there are thousands of miles of pipelines carrying the inexpensive clean burning fuel to millions of homes and businesses throughout North America.

With all of the advantages of natural gas it has a down side as well. Natural gas is odorless and extremely volatile. Earlier in its use, natural gas leaks were not readily detected. If the gas escaped outdoors it is harmlessly dissipated into the atmosphere. But when natural gas is collected or trapped in a structure, it cannot be detected by odor or sight and a spark could trigger a huge explosion.

To counter this disadvantage of natural gas, an odor resembling rotten eggs is added to the gas to make it noticeable in case of leaks. Despite making leaks easier to detect, there are still leaks that result in explosions.

On a crisp day in October of 1960, shoppers were looking for sales and at the display windows of the stores on Ouellette Avenue, Windsor, Ontario's main business avenue. The Metropolitan Store's 60 feet of glass windows displayed merchandise arranged to attract attention and entice shoppers in.

The Metropolitan Store, the largest department store in Windsor, was a favorite of the shoppers. It offered a variety of goods on two floors and a basement. A favorite part of the store was its lunch counter that took up a large portion of the rear of the ground floor. It was a gathering spot for many neighborhood residents and the food was very good.

The Metropolitan Store's location was ideal. It was on the busy avenue of Ouellette and it was across the street from the tunnel under the Detroit River connecting Detroit, Michigan, in the United States and Windsor, Ontario, in Canada. When cars pulled out of the tunnel the store was one of the first buildings they saw.

On October 25, 1960, about 150 customers and store clerks were in the Metropolitan Store. Several of them sat at the lunch counter eating a late lunch and chatting with friends over tea and coffee while children at the counter drank their cherry Cokes and spun around on the stools. Shoppers looked over the tables of sweaters on sale and others browsed women's apparel and children's clothes.

A couple from Windsor had finished a leisurely lunch in the store and started down the stairway to the basement where toys, sewing supplies and hardware were sold, when an ear shattering explosion shook the building and knocked them to the stairs. The lights went out, throwing them into darkness; they heard a rumbling as part of the cement block building collapsed. Then a thick choking dust filled the air.

On the street in front of the Metropolitan Store, the sixty feet of glass display windows blew out in a shower of sharp deadly shards. The glass struck people several yards from the building, lacerating the faces, arms and torso of people walking on the street near the Metropolitan Store. People laid along the street while blood flowed in the gutter.

The blast did the most damage in the rear of the store where a section of the ground floor, second floor and roof collapsed into the basement. The rear wall stood unsupported and in jeopardy of collapsing. Other than the

broken display windows and merchandise and glass strewn about, the front of the store was intact.

Some women and children staggered out the front door cut and bloodied, bones broken, but alive. Others less fortunate were trapped, some crushed, beneath the rubble of the ground and second floors. Many of the shoppers once leisurely enjoying their lunch at the lunch counter were now trapped below the rubble of the floors above. Worse were the customers and sale clerks in the basement who were crushed when the heavy lunch counter fell onto them.

Residents from the area and those working nearby were the first to respond to the explosion followed by police and the fire department. The rescuers ran across the shattered glass covering the street into the front of the store. They were not prepared for the horror that met them.

The rescuers groped through darkness and dust looking for the poor souls trapped in the building. The sounds of hell reverberated through the building; screams and moans from those trapped and a baby's muffled voice crying out "mama".

One man who had exited the Detroit/Windsor tunnel just as the explosion occurred, stopped his car and raced into the building and brought out two small boys, bloodied and in shock. He handed them over to a passerby and returned to the building. That same man helped several other injured people from the building.

Rescuers dug through the rubble with their bare hands in an effort to reach the victims. A firefighter drew on his strength to move a large section of debris to see a woman's arm protruding from a pile of bricks. He dug through the bricks with renewed urgency only to find a store mannequin, a scene repeated several times.

The rescue attempt had to be stopped for a while for fear the unsupported rear wall of the building might collapse. The wall was temporarily shored up so the rescue work could proceed.

Several of the emergency crew heard the cry of a baby beneath the wreckage and dug by hand until they found a toy doll crying, "Mama, mama."

On that day in a small twenty-foot by twenty-foot boiler room in the basement of the store, a plumber, electrician, the store manager and another store employee were in the process of installing a new gas furnace. Several months earlier the work to replace the old coal heating system had started and on that day the crew was going to connect the new furnace to the gas pipe.

The store manager, Joe Halford, who was badly burned in the explosion, said they had installed the new system and turned the gas on. They waited 15 minutes for the pipe to bleed air out of the system but no gas seemed to be coming from the pipe.

Then they disconnected a three-inch gas main from the meter and opened the valve to purge the air from the pipe. They thought only air was coming out but natural gas was escaping and accumulating in the boiler room at the rear of the store. A water heater in the basement ignited the gas and the resulting explosion tore through the two floors.

There were some small fires in the basement area that were quickly extinguished by the Windsor Fire Department; the majority of the damage was the result of the explosion.

Windsor's three major hospitals, Grace Hospital, Hotel Dieu Hospital and Metropolitan Memorial Hospital, called in all nurses and doctors to treat the victims of the blast. All ambulances in the city were sent to the scene of the disaster.

Over one hundred men, women and children were taken to the three hospitals with various injuries, some critical. Ten people who were pulled from the wreckage of the building were taken to the Windsor morgue.

FIVE DAYS IN HELL

Harry, a World War II veteran and retired Chicago sanitation worker, sat in his trailer on the city's south side. The trailer had been his home since his wife had passed away from breast cancer almost a decade ago.

Sitting in his reclining chair, Harry watched the weather report on a Chicago news broadcast. "It's hot and it's going to get hotter," the meteorologist reported.

The air-conditioner hadn't worked in a year and most of his windows either didn't open or still had the plastic taped on them to keep winter's cold out, so Harry sat in his under shorts, his old oscillating fan blowing on him, trying to cope with the heat. .

"Its going to be over 100 degrees today," he mumbled to himself as he reached for another beer.

A few days later Harry's son who lives near Detroit called one of his father's neighbors because his dad hadn't answered the phone. The neighbors realized they had not seen Harry since the hot spell started five days earlier. They went to check; his car was in the drive but he didn't respond to their knocks. They called the police.

When the officers forced the door, suffocating heat and the stench of death bellowed out of the trailer. One officer said he thought it must have been 150 degrees in the trailer.

They found Harry in his recliner, the fan sweeping back and forth blowing hot air, the TV still on and a full beer and three empties on the table to his left. Harry was dead.

Harry was one of the deaths attributed to the extreme heat that hung over Chicago, Illinois July 12- 16, 1995.

July is one of the hottest months in the Midwest but on those five days in 1995, several climatological factors came into play.

Interaction of high and low-pressure systems creates wind. If the wind is from the north it is usually a cooling Canadian breeze. If it originates in the south it is warm. But on those days in 1995, a high-pressure system stalled over the Chicago area. No wind was created.

County heat deaths will surpass 400

Another contributing factor is that a high-pressure system creates heat. The cooler air high in the atmosphere drops down towards the earth. As it drops it condenses and physics tells us when something is condensed it heats up. The high-pressure system was sending heated air towards Chicago with no wind to move it off.

The result was a five-day heat wave with temperatures in the high 90s and 100s. One day the temperature reached a blistering 106 degrees.

The human body is designed to adjust for changes in temperature. Our bodies are cooled in four basic ways, radiation, conduction, convection, and evaporation.

If the surrounding temperature is lower than our normal body temperature our bodies radiate heat to keep us cool. Our bodies have the ability to transfer heat to something else it comes into contact with, such as water in a bath or a dip in a lake. When a breeze, natural or from a fan, blows across our skin, heat is removed from our bodies by convection, and our body also cools itself by evaporation. When we sweat the moisture on our bodies evaporates and removes heat.

Wednesday, July 12 saw a temperature of 97 degrees, Thursday was an all time high of 106 degrees and 100 degrees was the high on Friday. The weekend brought more of the same, 98 on Saturday and Sunday it was 93 degrees.

For many Chicagoans in July, 1995, the heat wave was a bearable nuisance. They lived and worked in air-conditioned buildings, cooled off in Lake Michigan, swam in backyard pools, spent time in air-conditioned theaters and malls, and drank plenty of water to replenish the water their bodies lost. They were able to curtail strenuous work in the heat, did not drink alcoholic beverages to excess and were young enough for their bodies to adapt to the heat.

But many other Chicago residents were not as lucky. Not everyone had the luxury of air-conditioning and during the extended heat wave they left their homes to find public air-conditioned buildings. Unfortunately many people could not leave their homes because of illnesses or handicaps that kept them housebound. Some didn't want to leave because their neighborhoods were not safe and they were afraid to leave their homes. Others just didn't like to leave their homes.

Those remaining in their homes or apartments without air-conditioning sat in front of fans and opened windows hoping to catch a cross breeze. But there wasn't a breeze, and fans only moved around air too warm to cool the body by convection. Often they lived in apartment buildings surrounded by concrete streets and sidewalks. Unlike grass and trees that are cooling, the concrete absorbs heat and radiates it back.

With heat in excess of 100 degrees, people need to drink plenty of water to replenish the fluids their bodies lose from their sweat glands. Some people trapped in the heat were alcoholics who continued to drink to excess. While a cold beer on a hot day is thirst quenching, it is not good for your body. The alcohol of the beverage intensifies dehydration in the body tissues rather than replenishes it.

The social group most prone to the heat of the Chicago heat wave was the elderly. They are more susceptible to heat related illnesses for several reasons. The elderly tend to be taking more medications for a variety of conditions. The drugs they ingest may be helping them under normal conditions but when their bodies are extremely warm, the medications counteract their bodies' attempt to cool it. A diuretic medication commonly given to patients for heart ailments decreases the body's fluids which are needed to maintain a stable temperature.

City deaths in heat wave triple normal

Toll now at 436 and still rising

■ A heat warning system may curb death tolls. Sec. 2, pg. 1.

survived it not for the heat wave.

Older persons are also more affected by the heat because the hypothalamus, a small portion of the brain whose function is to sense when the body is overheating, works slower as we age and doesn't signal the heart to increase blood flow. And sweat glands degenerate over time and don't function as well in cooling the body.

These medical conditions can result in the body overheating and succumbing to heat stroke.

The symptoms of heat stroke are; headache, fatigue, confusion, and a body temperature approaching 107 degrees. If immediate action is not taken, the victim will become unconscious, slip into a coma and die.

Another factor which makes the elderly more susceptible to death during a heat wave like that which baked Chicago in 1995 is that they may not have anyone close by to check on them. Children have moved away, spouses have died, close friends have moved or passed away. Neighbors did not know their plight; they suffered in the heat alone and they died from the heat alone.

Chicago residents opened fire hydrants hoping the cool water would give them some reprieve from the heat. Almost 4,000 of the cities 48,000 hydrants had been opened, giving officials cause for concern if adequate pressure would be available in the event of a major fire. City crews were sent out to close and, in many cases, repair damage done to the hydrants. Residents upset with their work threw rocks and bricks at the crews. It was also reported that gunshots were fired at repair crew trucks.

As the heat wave continued from day to day, more people were found dead from heat related illness.

The Cook County Coroners Office reported that there are normally about 240 heat related deaths annually in the entire United States. By Saturday, July 15, 1995 the morgue had handled 54 heat related deaths. Refrigerated trailers were brought in to hold the bodies for autopsy. The number climbed to 116 the following day. By the time a cool front swept down from the north more victims were found. The total death toll related to the Chicago heat wave of 1995 was approximately 750 persons.

Most of the dead were elderly and those weakened by sickness and the heat exasperated their conditions. Others were homeless with no place to escape the oppressive heat.

Some deaths were indirectly related to the heat wave and others were heat related. Some heat related deaths were a woman who was driving with the rear window of her Ford Bronco open to try to get a breeze. The exhaust of the engine was sucked into the passenger compartment and asphyxiated

Chicago Tribune

Sunday, July 16, 1995

Chicagoland
Final
$1.50

Heat wave death toll soars
56 in Chicago area fall victim even as temperature dips

two three-year-old boys in the back seat. A couple was afraid to open their windows for fear a criminal would enter and died from heat stroke. Another woman who didn't like air-conditioning died with her air-conditioner still in the box in her basement.

In the aftermath of the 1995 Chicago heat wave, it was found that lack of access to air-conditioning was one of the largest contributors to the 750 deaths attributed to the heat. The Center for Disease control stated that those without access to air-conditioning stood a 49.8 % greater chance of dying. And those in a lower economic class were more likely to suffer from the effects of the heat wave because they could not afford air-conditioners or lived on the upper floors of apartment buildings where heat accumulated.

The climatological patterns which developed over the Midwest and specifically Chicago, were not necessarily unusual. A high-pressure system will often form and temperatures will rise above normal but the unusual feature of this weather pattern is that it stalled over the city and the oppressive temperatures remained for five days.

The City of Chicago and emergency preparedness departments around the world learned from this disaster. During heat emergencies, air-conditioned public buildings must be made available to all citizens, volunteers and government employees must go door to door looking for residents not able to cope with the conditions, fresh drinking water must be made available to the general public, and health officials must work to educate the community of the effects of excessive heat.

THE GREAT 1913 OHIO FLOOD

In March of 1913, a series of storms barreled across the mid section of the United States. The storms of high winds and torrential rainfall spawned several tornadoes that reeked havoc across the country.

In Omaha, Nebraska, a tornado swept through the city destroying homes in a swath a half of a mile wide and several miles long, killing 152 and injuring 330 others.

The killer storms moved on to Council Bluffs, Iowa, where twelve more men, women and children died.

The storms continued across the nation; in Chicago the storms and tornadoes destroyed fifty buildings killing at least six and injured dozens.

Two railroad firemen were killed in Chicago when a brick chimney was blown down and landed on the caboose in which they were riding.

Terre Haute, Indiana, was hit hard by the storms that rolled over the area in March of 1913. The tornadoes that ripped through the area killed over fifty people and wounded hundreds. The heavy rains that accompanied the storms fell at the rate of over 2 inches an hour causing the Wabash River

One of the tornadoes that devastated Omaha, Nebraska during the March of 1913 storms. From the NOAA Weather Service.

The destruction in Omaha following the storms. From the NOAA Weather Service.

to overflow its banks until the river was over 14 miles wide. Hundreds of houses and shops were damaged or destroyed leaving thousands homeless. Communication with the world outside the city was cut off when telephone and telegraph lines were downed, roads were impassable and the railroad track bed was washed away.

Dayton, Ohio, was especially hard hit by the storms. Dayton is the sixth largest city in the state and the home to Orville and Wilbur Wright's bicycle repair shop where the brothers developed the first propeller aircraft to successfully fly.

Some of the damage in Terre Haute, Indiana following the March 1913 storms. From the NOAA Weather Service.

Dayton was founded along the banks of the Great Miami River near where the Stillwater River, Mad River and Wolf Creek converge with the Great Miami.

It is said that Native Americans warned the city's founding fathers that the area was not a good location for a city because the river was prone to flooding. The advice was ignored and Dayton was established in the Great Miami River floodplain.

They should have listened to the wisdom of the Native Americans. The river overflowed its banks at least once every decade.

The storm system that marched across the country in 1913 reached Dayton on Friday March 21, 1913. It blasted the area with near hurricane velocity winds and heavy rain, yet the temperature was an unusually warm 60 + degrees.

On Saturday, Dayton area residents awoke to beautiful sunny skies until the next weather front came through with more severe winds dropping the temperature by 40 degrees. The rain soaked ground quickly froze in the sub freezing weather.

A third storm assaulted the area on March 23. The rains accompanying the storm fell over the entire Great Miami River watershed. The frozen ground couldn't absorb the rains so it flowed in torrents into the Great Miami and its tributaries.

Between 8 and 11 inches of rain fell over the watershed for over 24 hours swelling the Great Miami to a flood stage of 11.6 feet in Dayton, and it was still rising as waters upstream roared down.

Levees built in critical locations along the river were holding back the river but were in jeopardy of being breeched.

By March 25, the rains had so swelled the rivers that several of the levees could no longer hold it back. Alarms were sounded to warn the

The Dayton, Ohio business district during the flood of 1913. From the NOAA Weather Service.

people of the impending danger. By 5:30 in the morning, the river was over flowing its levees at a rate of 100,000 cubic feet per second.

A few hours later, the levees protecting the downtown Dayton area gave way. The violently fast moving water tore through the business district ripping buildings from their foundations and carrying anything in its path downstream. Horses still harnessed to wagons were carried away and smashed into buildings. Anyone who had not heeded the alarms was swept away by the vicious current to either drown or be battered by the debris caught in the flow.

The water in the downtown area crested at an amazing 20.1 feet in depth covering almost 15 square miles.

On Wednesday, the raging river ripped a fuel tank from its foundation sending it cascading along in the current. The tank smashed into a downtown building and burst into flames with a huge explosion. Buildings for several blocks caught on fire.

Other fires broke out throughout the city as gas lines broke, releasing the highly volatile vapors. Hundreds of people sheltering in the Beckel House Hotel climbed to the upper floors to escape the rising water only to become trapped when the hotel caught on fire.

People either not expecting the flood or not expecting it to be as bad as it was or not able to escape in time took refuge on top of roofs and climbed trees in an effort to save themselves.

THE GREAT 1913 OHIO FLOOD

250 FLOOD REFUGEES BURN TO DEATH

5 O'CLOCK **SPECIAL EDITION** *PERISH WHEN FLAMES DESTROY DAYTON HOTEL*

The Detroit Free Press OHIO FACES WORSE DISASTER

DETROIT, MICHIGAN, THURSDAY, MARCH 7, 1913, SIXTEEN PAGES

The storms and flooding at Dayton were some of the worst in the state, the floodwaters and fires practically destroyed the downtown area and 123 people were killed.

Dayton was not alone in the devastation as the entire state of Ohio fell victim to the storms of March of 1913. In Hamilton, almost one hundred people died as the swift waters of the Great Miami River rose to over 18 feet in some neighborhoods. In the larger city of Columbus, Ohio, over one hundred men, women and children were killed when the Scioto River breeched its levees and water rose to 17 feet deep.

The cities in northern Ohio were victimized by the storm as well. The Cuyahoga River at Cleveland, swelled by the heavy rain storms washed away docks, damaged ships, destroyed warehouses and other structures along the river.

The storms that assaulted Ohio in March of 1913 are known as the "Greatest Natural Disaster in Ohio History." The known death toll was 467 men, women and children, more than 40,000 homes flooded and thousands of horses and other animals killed.

THE 1925 THREE STATE TORNADO

The spring of the year always produces unsettled weather patterns but the tornado of 1925 that swept through three states is one for the record books. It set the record for remaining on the ground for an astonishing 219 continuous miles. Its time of 3.5 hours of continuous ground time was a record and, unfortunately, it set the record for the most fatalities from a single tornado, with 695 confirmed dead it is the deadliest tornado in the history of the United States.

On Wednesday, March 18, 1925, around 1:00 p.m., residents near Ellington, Missouri, reported that a storm like none they could remember was forming to the southwest. The sky turned black, and it was getting darker and darker until one o'clock in the afternoon was as black as midnight.

Most residents took shelter in basements or cellars, huddling in the darkness waiting for the storm to pass. When they heard the roar they compared to a locomotive pulling a string of cars up a steep grade, they knew it was a tornado!

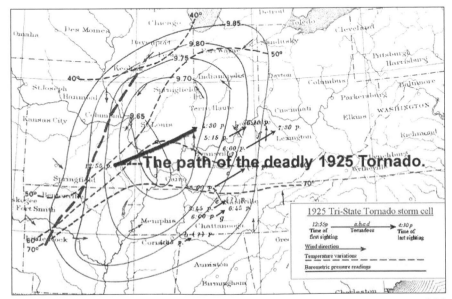

The path of the deadly 1925 Tornado.

GREAT LAKES DISASTERS

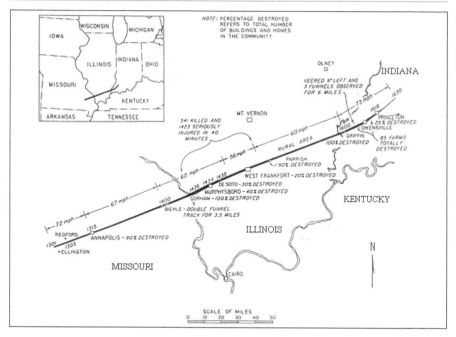

The same scenario was repeated in other Missouri towns as the tornado continued on its path striking the communities of Annapolis and Leadanna killing at least two.

Moving at an average speed of 62 miles per hour, the tornado blasted in to Bollinger County where it damaged two schools injuring 32 children. The storm continued through Cornwall, Biehle and Frohna, Missouri.

It is reported that at least eleven people in Missouri were killed by the twister.

The deadly tornado jumped the Mississippi River into southern Illinois. The town of Gorham was the first to feel the brunt of the storm. The entire town was destroyed and more than thirty were killed.

The killer swept down on the town of Murphysboro, Illinois, destroying a one hundred and twenty block section of the town and killing 204 people. Included in the destruction was the township high school. Seventeen students in the school were killed, scores were injured and the school was destroyed.

Not far from the high school, the Longfellow School was severely damaged with ten students killed. Five more students were killed when the Logan school was assaulted by the deadly storm.

In De Soto, Illinois, the tornado took aim on the village. There wasn't a store, house, church or school that did not receive damage. The small

142

THE 1925 THREE STATE TORNADO

Murphysboro, Illinois after the 1925 tornado.

village was devastated by the loss of 154 lives, killing 33 children in attendance at the De Soto school.

Illinois holds the dubious distinction of the most lives lost by a single tornado. On that fateful day in March, at least 613 men, women and children were killed by the tornado.

The Wabash River separating Illinois and Indiana was no match for the tornado. The storm barreled into Indiana reeking havoc in the southern corner of that state, disseminating any town unfortunate enough to be in its way.

The remains of the Longfellow school after the March 1925 tornado. NOAA Weather Service photograph.

Griffin was the first to be wiped out, then Owensville and Princeton. The tornado killed a minimum of seventy one people in Indiana before it dissipated at 4:30 p.m.

The Great Tri-State tornado of 1925, as it became to be known, killed at least 695 and injured 2,027 others.

The storm was one for the meteorological record books but the storm also set another

143

record; the most school-children killed in a single incident. Through the tri state area nine schools were damaged or destroyed killing a total of sixty nine children, including the record of thirty three children killed in one school when the deadly twister blasted the De Soto school.

The remains of a Model T after the 1925 tornado.

MIDWEST EXPRESS
FLIGHT 105

In 1948 the Kimberly-Clark Corporation established K-C Aviation. The Aviation branch of the company was used primarily to transport company executives and engineers from its Neenah, Wisconsin, headquarters to its mills around the country.

Kimberly-Clark is one of the nations leading manufacturers of a variety of paper products, its premier products being Kleenex and Kotex. The aviation division grew from its small corporate fleet of propeller planes to a fleet of jet aircraft flying under the name of Midwest Express Airlines.

Midwest Express Airlines was a small regional carrier that flew out of Milwaukee's General Billy Mitchell Field and flew to a variety of locations including Hartsfield International Airport in Atlanta, Georgia.

On September 6, 1985, Midwest Express Airlines Flight 105, a McDonnell Douglas DC 9-14 arrived at Milwaukee from Madison, Wisconsin, at 2:41 pm. Following protocol, the first officer Bill Weiss contacted the Milwaukee tower to request an instrument flight rule to Atlanta.

The Captain, Dan Martin, made contact with the Midwest Express dispatch in Appleton, Wisconsin, and received flight information for Atlanta. The weather report indicated possible thunderstorms en route and alternative landing sights were selected in case the aircraft could not land in Atlanta due to weather.

Captain Martin and Midwest dispatch determined flight 105 would require 19,500 pounds of fuel. It was more than necessary for a flight to Atlanta but it allowed for possible diversions around the thunderstorms. Other details of flight 105 were discussed before the captain signed the dispatch release.

The pilot and co-pilot completed the "Before Engine Start" checklist and started the Pratt & Whitney JT8D-7 engines. The flight crew then commenced the "After Engine Start" checklist.

With the engines running and all systems in the cockpit looking good, the first officer called the control tower requesting clearance to taxi to runway 19R.

The cockpit of a McDonnell-Douglas DC-9. Wiki Commons *photograph* collection.

Both the pilot and co-pilot on the flight had earned a captain rating. They rotated the captain and first officer responsibilities on every other flight. Captain Martin had 5,100 total flight hours and Captain Weiss 5,197 hours. Captain Weiss also was previously a F-4 pilot with the United States Air Force.

Following airline regulations, a Midwest service agent walked around the craft to make sure all doors were secured. In the cabin, flight attendants were instructing the passengers on how to buckle their seat belts, where the emergency exits were located and that their seats would double as a floatation device in the unlikely event of a water landing.

The taxi checklist was completed to insure that the aircraft was operating at its peak performance prior to departing the gate.

Captain Martin radioed to the control tower, "Milwaukee Midex 4/105 on 19R". He was told to "Position and Hold". The flight crew performed the "Before Take Off" checklist and reported no discrepancies. At 3:20 pm, Midwest Express Flight 105 was cleared for take off. Captain Martin acknowledged the clearance.

The McDonnell Douglas DC 9-14 was first introduced in 1965 with 976 units of various configurations built through 1982. The $41.5 million to $48.5 million aircraft was specifically designed for the short-range,

Milwaukee jet crash kills 31

DC-9 falls
just after
taking off

frequent flight market. The aircraft was powered by two Pratt & Whitney JT8D-7 turbofan engines mounted at the rear on the fuselage capable of a cruising speed of 561 miles per hour.

K-C Aviation, a wholly owned subsidiary of Kimberly-Clark Corporation, the parent company of Midwest Express, purchased the DC 9-14 in 1983. The unit had been built in 1968 and had spent the first years of its career flying for two South American airlines.

The airliner was designed to carry 90 passengers in five seats across the cabin with a single aisle, yet on the September 6th flight from Milwaukee non-stop to Atlanta there were only 27 passengers, two pilots, and two flight attendants.

The roll off of Flight 105 was normal. When the aircraft reached 140 knots, flight 105 lifted off the runway 4,200 feet from the beginning of the runway. The rate of climb was as the pilots of the DC 9-14 expected and by the time they were 450 feet off the ground they were 7,600 feet down the runway.

The air traffic controller heard over the radio a loud bang and the engine noise seemed to decrease.

"What the @#$% was that?" Captain Martin asked.

"Midex 105, turn left heading 175," the tower instructed.

The tower next heard the pilot say to the co-pilot, "What do we have here, Bill?"

The first officer responded to the towers instructions, "Midex 105, Roger. We've got an emergency here!"

Witnesses on the ground reported they saw flames and smoke coming from the right engine. The witnesses also told of hearing one or more loud "bangs" similar to the firing of a shotgun.

Flight 105 continued to climb for a few seconds to an estimated 700 feet, before the aircraft's wings rocked up and down and the nose of the DC 9-14 lowered to a near level attitude.

The airplane rolled suddenly to a 90 degree bank with the wings of the aircraft nearly perpendicular to the ground. The aircraft went into a stall and the nose of the airplane pointed down towards the ground.

Flight 105 began a slow spin to the right revolving one to one and half times.

Midwest Express Flight 105 crashed to the ground 1,680 feet southwest of the end of runway 19R. The two pilots, flight attendants and all 27 passengers were killed.

The aircraft broke into pieces on impact and the entire wreckage field burst into flames.

The 440th Air Force Reserve fire department saw the impact and responded immediately followed by the airport fire department, the 128th Air National Guard fire department and the Oak City fire department. The fire suppression equipment was quickly implemented and the flames were controlled and extinguished promptly.

As soon as the wreckage had cooled, half of the bodies of the dead were removed and taken to the Milwaukee County Medical Examiner's office. The others were found amongst the wreckage over the next several hours. The result of the autopsy was that all of those on board Flight 105 were killed by,"multiple massive injuries to the head, torso and extremities."

The National Transportation Safety Board (NTSB) launched an investigation into the cause of the accident. After an examination of the right engine, it was found that a removable compressor stage spacer had broken and the 9th and 10th compressor blades were ejected from the engine.

The sudden loss of power of the right engine during the climb caused the aircraft to veer to the right. The DC 9-14 then lost power in the left engine and lost the thrust necessary to obtain flight. The NTSB was not able to determine the cause of the left engine power loss.

The NTSB determined the spacer was cracked and the crack should have been discovered at the engine overhaul two years earlier. They recommended that removable spacers on all Pratt & Whitney JT8D-7 engines be replaced with a one-piece integral sleeve spacer.

Air Safety investigators said the aircraft had the ability to recover from a loss of one engine on take off and maintain a level flight configuration and it would not require any special skill or strength on the part of the pilot. The flight recorder indicated that Captain Martin did begin the proper corrective action but for some reason discontinued the action.

The NTSB also found that Midwest Express Airlines had not properly instructed the pilots in the corrective actions needed in such an event.

The passengers killed aboard Midwest Express Flight 105 included 21 people from Georgia, five residents of Wisconsin, and one man from North Carolina. Both Captain Martin and Captain Weiss lived in Appleton, Wisconsin, and flight attendants Amy Bain and Sharon Herb were from Milwaukee.

OHIO PENITENTIARY FIRE

A prison is usually not a place most of us choose to be. It's designed not to be a pleasant place to be, yet thousands of criminals, both men and women, end up housed in one of the state and federal penitentiaries throughout North America each year.

Prisons today are much more humane than their counterparts of the past. The descriptions of the inhuman treatment of prisoners laboring on chain gangs and of living in filthy, overcrowded prisons in America's past linger to haunt today's prison authorities.

In the early years of the 1800s, the population of Columbus, Ohio, was booming. Along with the influx of hard working, God fearing people, the criminal element in the community was growing as well.

To deal with the rise in thieves, rapists, murderers and con men, Columbus needed to build a new penitentiary.

A new Ohio Penitentiary, built in 1834 on Spring Street in the city, was designed to be large enough to incarcerate the prison population for many decades to come. The new prison would have all of the modern conveniences available in 1834, unlike the old prison that was built in 1813 and was much too inadequate to meet their current needs.

The Ohio Penitentiary in Columbus, Ohio. Courtesy of the Ohio Historical Society.

149

Conditions in the prison reflected the principle that a prison was a place of punishment not rehabilitation. Inmates slept on straw mattresses on the floor, ate meager meals, and were forced to work in prison industries. Prisoners were frequently subject to diseases caused by the unhygienic conditions, such as the 1849 epidemic of cholera that killed 121 inmates.

Prisoners held on death row awaited their appointment with the executioner. The condemned walked the steps of the gallows to be hung by their neck until 1897 when prison authorities installed an electric chair.

The prison population grew beyond expectations. It was always overcrowded but by the 1930s the "Ohio Pen," as it was known, designed to house 1,500 inmates was the home to 4,300 prisoners.

Some infamous American criminals were incarcerated in the Ohio State Penitentiary.

Confederate General John H. Morgan, was held in the prison during the Civil War. The General was known for the 1863 "Morgan's Raid" in which he lead Confederate troops against the Union army into Kentucky, Indiana and Ohio. It was the deepest that Confederate troops penetrated into the northern states during the war.

George "Bugs" Moran was famous for battling Al Capone for control of Chicago's illegal liquor trade during the prohibition era. He lived a life

The interior of the "Ohio Pen" showing the ranges. Courtesy of the Ohio Historical Society.

OHIO PENITENTIARY FIRE

The aftermath of the prison fire showing the destruction. Courtesy of the Ohio Historical Society.

of opulence and wealth off the money he illegally earned, but he fell out of favor and blew through his money. He resorted to less high profile crimes to survive. In 1946 Bugs Moran was found guilty of robbery and served ten years in the Ohio Penitentiary in Columbus.

One of the better-known inmates of the Ohio Pen was Dr. Sam Sheppard. In 1954, the Cleveland area physician was accused of murdering his pregnant wife as she lay in their bed. He denied the allegations and in a highly publicized trial he was found guilty and sentenced to the Ohio Penitentiary at Columbus. He served almost ten years of his sentence when he was granted a new trial in which he was found innocent. The television show and movie, "The Fugitive" is loosely based on the Sheppard case.

Shortly before 5:30 p.m. on April 21, 1930, while the inmates were being locked into their cells following dinner, smoke could be smelled and seen in sections G and H of the Prison.

In sections G and H there were six ranges, or levels. There were 17 cells per range, and 4 men housed in each cell. There were over eight hundred men in the sections being filled with smoke. Shortly after the smoke was discovered, flames were seen.

At the time, the prison was undergoing a renovation on a cellblock built in 1876 and temporary wood scaffolding had been erected in the section of cells. Somehow a fire started on the wood scaffolding and the blaze rose to the wood timber roof of the cellblock under renovation. The fire, fanned by a stiff breeze, quickly spread to the roof of the adjoining cellblock containing sections G and H.

The open corridors of sections G and H acted as a raceway for the blaze. The conflagration roared through the ranges, consuming any combustible material it encountered.

Over eight hundred inmates housed in the section screamed as their cells filled with thick, black, acrid smoke and red-hot embers showered down on them from above.

The inmates screamed for the guards to unlock the cell doors. But the guards, thinking it might be a ruse by the inmates to escape, refused to release them.

As thick choking smoke filled the cellblock and burning fragments rained down from the roof, the prisoners pleaded to be released from the inferno. The captain of the guards stood by fearing an escape and refused to open the cells.

Finally, guards William Baldwin and Thomas Little took it upon themselves to do something. They went to the guardroom and physically took the keys from the Range Captain and began unlocking cells.

Each cell had to be unlocked individually; a mechanism to open all doors at once had not been installed in this section of the prison.

As convicts, choking and gasping for breath, staggered from their cells towards the safety of the prison yard, Baldwin and Little climbed up the stairway to the next range and continued to quickly open cell doors. Several prisoners helped in the rescue efforts by opening cell doors with fire axes and carrying men too overcome by the smoke to safety.

Guard Little, choking in the dense suffocating smoke and the intense heat of the fire, fell to the floor after unlocking the last cell on the fourth

THE WEATHER
Partly cloudy and
colder tonight—Wednes-
day fair and colder.

THE LOWELL SUN

6 O'CLOCK

ESTABLISHED 1878   LOWELL MASS. TUESDAY APRIL 22 1930   18 PAGES TWO CENTS

PENITENTIARY FIRE STUNS NATION

Lowell May Reach 100,000 Mark

OHIO PENITENTIARY FIRE

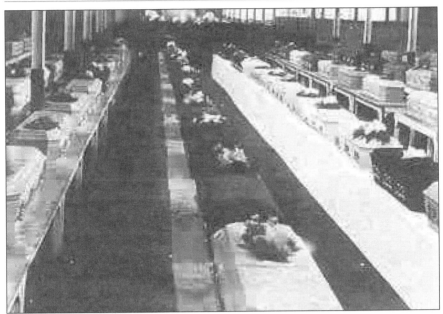

The caskets of the dead prisoners lined up in the Ohio State Fairgrounds. Courtesy of the Ohio Historical Society.

range. He was picked up by inmates and carried out to fresh air. Baldwin collapsed on the first range and inmates assisted him to safety.

Some inmates ran back and forth into the burning building to carry men out. Inmates carried their comrades suffering from smoke inhalation to the prison yard only to watch them lay on the grass and die. Soon the yard was filled with the corpses of the convicts that succumbed to the fire.

The heavy timbers of the roof were weakened by the flames and collapsed, trapping and burning the convicts housed on the upper ranges. Their screams of terror could be heard in the prison yard but it wasn't long before they fell silent.

At the height of the fire, 140 firefighters were on the scene with eight pump trucks supplying twenty-three hoses.

The inmates in the yard were overcome by the carnage surrounding them. They were angry. They wanted to know why they were not immediately released when it was obvious the section house was on fire. But they were left locked in their cells to die a painful, terrifying death.

They took out their frustrations on the fire department trying to extinguish the flames. Rocks were thrown at the fire fighters, fire hoses were cut, and some fire fighters attacked.

Fire fighters dragged their hoses into the burning building but were unable to help the men housed on the upper ranges because their hoses wouldn't reach that far.

All Ohio Penitentiary guards, city, county and state police officers were called in to quell the disturbance in the prison yard and to surround the prison to prevent convicts from escaping. Two army troops and 100 Ohio National Guardsmen were called in to bolster the police and prison guards. Guards high above the grounds trained their sub-machine guns on all of the entrances to the prison. The guards, police and military troops had instructions to shoot to kill.

Within three and half hours, the fire was under control. The prisoners standing in the cold night air eventually calmed and followed the guards' instructions to peacefully assemble in the dining hall.

The bodies of the dead were arranged in rows on the grass of the prison yard before they were moved to a makeshift morgue in an exhibition hall at the state fair grounds.

Most of the deaths occurred on the top levels of the cellblock. Of the 272 inmates housed on the top two floors, only 13 escaped. The rest of the men died as a result of breathing the toxic smoke, were crushed when the roof collapsed and/or were burned to death while still locked in their cells.

A federal investigation into the cause of the blaze and how prison officials handled it was launched. The report stated that Warden Thomas should have reacted quicker to the plight of the prisoners. He admitted he did not order the cells opened rather he first sent a guard with keys to the main gate to open up for the fire department then stood outside the wall, shotgun in hand, waiting for convicts trying to escape.

A year after the fire, two convicted murderers, who were part of a convict work crew, admitted that they had intentionally set the fires. They had put lit candles near piles of rags on the scaffolding. After the workers left, the candles would burn down and ignite the rags. They hoped the fire would divert the attention of the guards and they could escape in the confusion.

The deaths of 319 inmates and the 130 that were severely injured in the Ohio Penitentiary fire of April 21, 1930, remains to this day the worst disaster in the history of the American penal system.

NORTH LAKE
MINE DISASTER

Women and children stood around the fires trying to warm themselves in the cold November night air. Some sobbed, some openly cried, some prayed, but all suspected, but didn't want to admit that their husbands, sons, fathers or brothers might be dead.

The women and children of North Lake, a small mining community near Ishpeming in Michigan's Upper Peninsula, stood a vigil for their men. Their men were trapped 1,060 feet below the surface in the Cleveland-Cliffs Iron Company's Barnes-Hecker iron ore mine.

The tiny community of North Lake, west of the city of Ishpeming, Michigan, had grown up around the mine where about 150 men worked.

The mine site was situated near a wet swampy area. To eliminate the possibility of the surface water seeping into the mine, the swamp had to be drained. Once the water had been drained off and the surface dried out, the mining operations started.

The surface water had been drained but from the beginning the mine was known as a "wet" mine and the ore brought out was referred to as soup because of the mixture of ore and ground water. Pumps in the mine withdrew any water that seeped into it. When mining began, the pumps removed over 3,000 gallons per minute but the amount later dropped to about 700 gallons per minute.

On November 3, 1926, the day shift of 57 men had been lowered down the single shaft into the mine for their day's labor. The men were working on the ore vein on all levels of the mine.

Around 11:20, as the lunch hour approached, five men were being lifted to the surface. Just short of the surface they heard a disturbing low rumble from below, then a sudden blast of air shot up the shaft lifting the cage up several feet and blowing out their lanterns.

They knew what had happened, there had been a cave-in down in the mine.

The cave-in occurred in an offshoot from the main shaft. On the surface, an indentation approximately 300 feet long and 200 feet wide and almost 60 feet deep appeared in the once swampy area.

The rain that had fallen in the area had partially filled the swamp and the water seeping through the ground weakened the material that made up the bottom of the swamp above the shaft and it collapsed into the offshoot some 1,600 feet from the main shaft. There were no men working in the offshoot.

The first level of the mine suddenly filled with a muddy and sandy slurry. The water and mud rapidly flowed through the shaft tearing the timber shaft supports from the walls. The sludge poured down the lift shaft flooding the lower level of the mine. The muck rose until it inundated the second level and continued to rise higher in the lift shaft.

Three men, Jack Hanna, Joseph Mackee and Wilfred Willis were near the lift shaft on the second level of the mine. At the sound of the rumbling and the rush of air, they began to run to the lift shaft. They frantically rang for the lift cage to no avail.

Willis momentary questioned if he should start to climb the 800 feet up or go down to the third level just 200 feet down.

As a torrent of muddy water flowed down the shaft from above the three men grabbed the ladder lining the lift shaft and started climbing. They were 800 feet from the surface, 800 feet from safety.

Willis was first to the ladder and climbed as the mucky water and debris surged down around him. He yelled to his companions and looked down towards them. He saw them wallowing in the mud. The ladder had collapsed and they fell into the rising quagmire.

The twenty-three year old raced up the ladder with redoubled effort as the mud rose in the shaft, lapping at his boots. If he relented he would be sucked into the black seething caldron of mud and debris. Completely exhausted, Willis reached the surface after a ten minute frantic climb.

The lift shaft of the Barnes-Hecker mine was dug 1,060 feet into the earth. The muddy water and debris rose to 186 feet from the surface.

Rescuers started down the ladder but were turned back by sludge blocking the shaft. It would have to be pumped out before any attempt at rescue could be made. Although the rescue crew knew their efforts were not rescue, they knew the men in the mine had either drowned or suffocated in the mud. They were on a mission of body recovery so the families of the dead miners could provide a proper burial.

Under floodlights, men worked through the night erecting a bailer to dig out the mud in the shaft, while another group rushed to install a pump and system of pipes to drain the crater left by the cave-in that was filling once again.

NORTH LAKE MINE DISASTER

As the bailer worked to clear the mud and debris that blocked the shaft, the rescuers uncovered the bodies of five miners. The five were probably near the shaft and ran towards it when the earth rumbled. But they were overtaken by the sludge or killed by rocks falling from the roof of the shaft.

Later, as water receded in the mine's vertical shaft, rescuers were able to almost reach the first level. They reported seeing bodies of men caught up in the muck as it swirled draining down into the next level. There was nothing they could do but watch the bodies disappear down the shaft.

Fifty-two men died deep in the earth in the Cleveland-Cliffs Iron Company's Barnes-Hecker mine including William E. Hill, the Marquette County Mine Inspector. Mr. Hill was making a required monthly inspection of the mine.

In days, the water and mud had descended to the 400 foot mark in the lift shaft. A respected group of mining engineers was assembled to determine what course of action should be taken. After several days of bailing the shaft and encountering blockages, the engineers unanimously decided the bodies of the men trapped deep in the mine could not be recovered and the mine should be permanently sealed.

Ten of the miner's bodies were recovered from the Barnes-Hecker mine. Wilfred Willis was the only man in the mine to survive the cave-in.

The women and children standing a mournful vigil at the Cleveland-Cliffs Iron Company's Barnes-Hecker mine wept for their husbands and fathers. Most of the miners that were trapped and drowned in the muck and mud were married and with children and most of the families lived in North Lake. In a matter of minutes, almost all of the women and children of the little village of North Lake became widows and orphans.

The cave-in at the Barnes-Hecker mine and the deaths of the 52 men is the worst single disaster in Michigan mining history.

THE OUR LADY OF THE ANGELS SCHOOL FIRE

Decmber 1, 1958, in the Our Lady of the Angels, school began like the first day of December in most schools. Thanksgiving day decorations came down and Christmas decorations hung.

In Sister Mary Seraphic Kelley's 4th grade class, the outline of the students hands made into turkeys and pictures of the Pilgrims sharing a meal with the Native Americans were taken down. Meanwhile Sister Mary Clare Therese Champagne hung pictures of baby Jesus lying in the manger in her fifth grade classroom to celebrate the birth of Jesus Christ.

The Our Lady of Angels school that housed 1,635 students in grades Kindergarten through Eighth was located at 909 North Avers Avenue in the Humboldt Park area on the West Side of Chicago, in a predominately Italian neighborhood.

The north wing of the brick school building was originally built in 1910 with a church on the first floor and the school on the second. In 1939 the south wing of the school and a new separate church were built. The first floor of the north wing was renovated into additional school classrooms. In 1951 the north and south wings were connected by an annex.

The Our Lady of the Angels school. Courtesy of olafire.com.

Firemen carry students down ladders from the second floor while other firemen train their hoses on the blaze. Courtesy of olafire.com.

As the December 1, 1958, school day came to a close, the classrooms performed their normal end of day duties. One of the daily routines was for one or two students from each classroom to carry the classroom trash can down the stairwells to the basement. The students emptied the can into cardboard boxes near the boiler and later a custodian would burn the waste paper in the boiler firebox.

Three 8th grade girls were climbing the stairway, returning to their classroom on the second floor. When they reached the second floor of the north wing they encountered smoke in the corridor. They quickly ran to their classroom and told their teacher, Sister Helaine O'Neill. Sister O'Neill directed her students to line up in preparation for evacuation but when she opened the door she discovered the smoke filled hallway was impassable.

The school custodian discovered a fire in the basement. He told two boys emptying trash to run back to their classrooms and tell their teachers to get their students out of the building and to warn everyone else. He ran to the rectory, told them to call the fire department, then ran back to the school to help with the evacuation.

The fire had started in the northeast stairwell of the north building. The wood stairwell quickly caught fire and burned as the open stairwell acted as a chimney funneling the smoke, flames and super heated air shot upward like the flames of a blowtorch.

THE OUR LADY OF THE ANGELS SCHOOL FIRE

The fire door at the first floor was closed so the smoke and fire did not enter the first floor corridor or the classrooms on that floor. The fire door at the second floor was propped open allowing the fire to gain access. The superheated smoke raced down the 35 yard long second floor corridor igniting anything combustible.

A fire alarmed alerted all of the classrooms to immediately exit the building. The students in the south building could smell the thick acrid smoke but were able to get out safely. The classrooms on the first floor of the north building felt the heat and choked on the smoke but ran from the building to the outdoor fresh air. The fire was contained in the north building.

The fire department arrived with sirens blaring. They quickly surveyed the situation and set up their equipment to train hoses on the stairwell and the second floor. Firemen hurriedly propped their ladders against the building to rescue the children hanging out the windows screaming for help.

A teacher in a classroom on the second floor directed her students to crawl on their hands and knees to the front staircase. They crawled and rolled down the stairs and out the door to safety.

Other students and teachers were not so fortunate. To reach the only fire escape in the building, students would need to pass through the corridor. Students screamed in panic when they realized they were trapped in their classrooms. The corridor was impassable

Some ran to the windows and jumped out the windows, some fell and others were pushed the twenty-five feet to the crushed gravel and concrete

An aerial view of the school blaze. Courtesy of olafire.com.

A fireman carries a young boy from the school. Courtesy of olafire.com.

below. Firemen found the children laying at the base of the building with broken bones and twisted limbs, some children were killed in the fall.

The fire climbed the pipe raceway, an area for pipes and electrical cables to run from the basement to the attic above the second floor. The wood roof timbers caught fire in the intense heat of the blaze.

The flames burned away at the sturdy timbers until they could no longer hold the load and a large section of the burning roof collapsed down on the classrooms below.

The students and teachers caught in rooms 208, 209, 210, 211, and 212 received the brunt of the devastation of the blaze as the burning roof fell down on them.

In Sister Mary St. Canice Lyng's seventh grade class in room 208, she and 13 of her students were found dead. Two eighth grade students in room 209 died in the blaze, while in room 210 Sister Mary Seraphica Kelley and her 27 fourth grade students succumbed to the effect of the smoke and heat of the burning school. Twenty-four eighth grade students in room 211 were killed and Sister Mary Clare Therese Champagne, died in room 212 with twenty-seven of her fifth grade students.

A young girl is rescued from the burning school by the fire department. Courtesy of olafire.com.

THE OUR LADY OF THE ANGELS SCHOOL FIRE

Within an hour and a half the fire was brought under control and suppressed. After the blaze was put out, firemen found children overcome by the toxic smoke huddled in groups beneath the windows. Some children were found still sitting at their desks. The firemen now had the unenviable task of removing the bodies of the children killed in the fire.

Eighty-seven students and three teaching nuns were killed and over one hundred were injured on that December day in 1958 in the blaze that ran rampant through the north wing of the Our Lady of Angels

The burned out second floor corridor. The path to the only fire escape. Courtesy of olafire.com.

school. Five more children died from their injuries in the following days bring the total deaths to 92 children and three teachers, making it one of the deadliest school disasters in America's history.

Authorities investigating the stairwell where the fire originated. Courtesy of olafire.com.

As soon as possible, investigators from the fire department and arson investigators from the Chicago Police Department swarmed the building looking for a cause of the blaze. They determined the fire had started in the basement stairwell of the old north wing. A 30-gallon trash can was located there and it was suspected that was the spot someone had intentionally set the

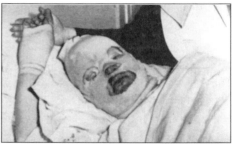

A child recovers in the hospital after being badly burned in the school fire. Courtesy of olafire.com.

fire. A theory was presented that possibly a youngster smoked a cigarette when he/she was sent to empty the classroom trash can and threw the lit cigarette butt in the can at the base of the stairs.

A fifth grade boy at the school confessed to setting the fire and to setting numerous other fires in the community, although he later recanted his confession of causing the school fire. Neither the boy or anyone else has ever been brought up on charges in the deadly fire at the Our Lady of Angels school.

A row of dead waiting to be claimed by their families. Courtesy of olafire.com.

PORT HURON
TUNNEL EXPLOSION

Freshwater is a valuable commodity. Countries have fought wars over it, residents of some countries draw their drinking water from the same rivers that contain human and animal wastes, and water starved western states covet the trillions of gallons of fresh water in the Great Lakes. Yet those of us living around the Great Lakes all too often take our good fortune for granted.

In the past, man has used the Great Lakes as a sewer and as a place to get rid of industrial wastes. Both the Canadian and United States governments have made great strides in regulating what is allowed to flow into the lakes. Their job is not yet done but lakes and rivers feeding them are now much cleaner.

More Michigan cities than any of the other states that surround the Great Lakes get their drinking water from the Lakes. The quality of the water is largely dependent on the location of the cities water intake. Water taken from the lakes near more populated areas, or more industrialized

A postcard showing the entrance to the St. Clair Tunnel. The tunnel was in operation for 104 years.

A illustration of Alfred Beach's Tunneling Shield in use digging the St. Clair Railroad tunnel in 1890. From the Port Huron Museum.

areas, requires more chemical treatment to remove impurities and bring it into acceptable standards.

The City of Detroit and its surrounding suburbs in the late 1960s was growing with no reason to suspect the sprawling metropolitan area would not continue to gain in population. Along with the increase in population, the area needed to augment its infrastructure to meet the demands of the future. The need for fresh water was on the top of the list of needs.

A new and state of the art water treatment plant was planned to service the metropolitan area. It would be built in Fort Gratiot Township, just north of Port Huron, Michigan.

The Fort Gratiot location was selected to take advantage of the clean fresh water of southern Lake Huron. A tunnel would be dug five miles under the lake to a location where the water was so pure it would require very little purifications treatment.

Water south of the Lake Huron site, the St. Clair River, Lake St. Clair and the Detroit River were lined on both the United States and Canadian sides with chemical plants and other industrial facilities, and municipal sewage treatment plants and storm sewers emptied into the waterway making the water not as pure as the Lake Huron location.

PORT HURON TUNNEL EXPLOSION

Construction began in 1968 on the $121 million water intake tunnel. The tunnel would be 16 feet in diameter by six miles long, five miles of which would be under the lake, dug 200 feet below the bottom of the lakebed. When completed, the tunnel would be capable of drawing 1.2 billion gallons of water per day.

Just a few miles south of the water tunnel is the site of the first railroad tunnel to be dug beneath a river and connect two countries. The St. Clair Tunnel opened in 1891 and ran below the St. Clair River between Port Huron, Michigan and Sarnia, Ontario.

The Grand Trunk Railroad built the tunnel at a cost of $2.7 million to replace the slow and costly process of crossing the river by ferry. Trains traveling on the busy Toronto, Ontario, and Chicago, Illinois, route had to stop at the St. Clair River, load the railcars onto the ferry, cross the river then re-assemble the train on the other side.

When the tunnel, measuring 19 feet 10 inches in diameter was dug, it was a technological feat for its time. It was the first time engineer Alfred Beach's "Tunneling Shield" was used. Two crews, one from the Canadian side and the other from the United States side dug towards each other and met near the middle.

The tunnel began operations in 1891 during the era of steam locomotives. Because of toxic fumes from burning coal in the locomotive's firebox, tunnel traffic was converted to electric trains only in 1907. The

The construction of the cofferdam in Lake Huron. Shown are only half of the 48 foot circular cells sunk to the lake bottom. When the remaining bines were sunk the center circle was pumped dry. From the Port Huron Museum.

use of electric trains was continued until 1958 when diesel electric locomotives began operations in the tunnel.

The St. Clair River Tunnel carried cargo and passengers beneath the St. Clair River for 104 years when it was closed and a new tunnel was opened. The new tunnel measures 27 feet 6 inches and will serve the railroad industry for decades to come.

To build the new water intake tunnel, a consortium of contractors was assembled under the name of Greenfield and Associates, which was made up of Greenfield Construction Company, Inc., Rocco Ferrara & Company, Inc., S.A. Healy Company, and the J.F. Shea Company.

The construction engineers determined that two crews should be used to dig the tunnel. One crew would dig the horizontal shaft from shore while another crew would be responsible to dig the vertical offshore shaft down to meet the horizontal shaft.

The shore crew would first bore a vertical elevator shaft 230 feet down into the shale rock, then a tunnel boring machine would dig an almost horizontal shaft six miles to the point it would meet the vertical water intake shaft.

On the lakeside of the project, a vertical shaft would be drilled in 47 feet of water, through 30 feet of clay and sand sediment and 100 feet of shale rock. But work on the lakeside end was troubled from the start.

Construction workers install the corrugated air duct in the horizontal shaft of the Detroit Metropolitan Water Service water intake tunnel in Fort Gratiot, Michigan. From the Port Huron Museum.

PORT HURON TUNNEL EXPLOSION

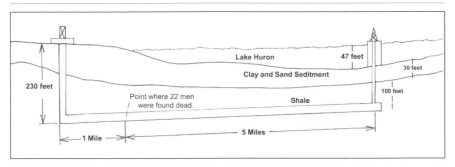

The plan was to construct seven circular metal cells each 48 feet in diameter and filled with rock and sand. The cells would be sunk to the bottom of the lake in a circular configuration to create a watertight cofferdam in the center. When the water was pumped out of the center, a dry environment was created for the drilling to be done. The drilling rig would be mounted on the tops of the cells.

But the circular cells became a problem. They were sunk to the lake bottom but they kept sinking deeper into the soft muddy sediment layer. To prevent the cells from settling further, refrigeration units were placed in the sediment to cool and solidify the soil and make it more stable.

But problems continued to plague the lakeside end of the project. In 1969, one of the seven cells collapsed requiring weeks of work to rebuild it. In 1970 and 1971, violent Lake Huron storms damaged several of the cells, setting the drilling of the lakeside vertical shaft further behind.

On the shore side of the project, work progressed very well. The vertical elevator shaft was sunk and the elevator mechanism was installed to carry the men up and down and to remove the spoils as the horizontal shaft was dug.

The boring equipment cut the horizontal shaft through the shale the distance of six miles then the "Tunnel Stiffs", as the men working the tunnel called themselves, began pouring the concrete liner of the tunnel.

By December 13, 1971, the tunneling project was just weeks from being finished. The onshore horizontal shaft was dug through the shale and the concrete liner was poured from the intake end of the tunnel five miles back towards shore.

The tunnel crew was preparing the concrete forms about one mile from the shore end of the tunnel while at the cofferdam end the lake crew was drilling a 23-inch ventilation shaft down through the sediment and shale. The two crews had not communicated with each other so neither was aware of what the other was doing.

SUNDAY
DECEMBER 12, 1971

PRICE 25 CENTS

THE TIMES HERALD

WEATHER
Cloudy Today
And Tonight

(Details on
Page 6A)

PORT HURON, MICHIGAN

Serving The Entire Thumb And River Districts   *Member Of The Gannett Group*

17 Killed, Others Feared Dead In Gas Explosion At Tunnel

The 23-inch ventilation shaft would later be widened for the water intake. The 23-inch bit slowly chewed through the shale rock breaking through the concrete liner of the horizontal shaft at 1:50. The crew tried to withdraw the bit but it was stuck in the shaft.

At 3:11 pm the crew decided that rather than fight with the stuck bit trying to bring it back up the bore hole, they would release it and allow it to fall into the horizontal shaft and retrieve it later.

The shale the bit bored through is called Antrim shale; almost the entire state of Michigan sits on a shelf of Antrim shale. The shale is well known for containing pockets of methane gas created by vegetation being trapped in the layer hundreds of thousands of years ago. The vegetation decays creating methane gas. The pockets are of varying size, the largest and most profitable to harvest pocket is in the northern counties of the Lower Peninsula where several thousand wells collect the natural gas for household and industrial use.

As the 23-inch bit bored the ventilation hole at the intake end of the tunnel, it apparently opened a pocket of gas. The colorless and odorless gas seeped into the tunnel during the period from when the bit broke through into the tunnel and when the cofferdam crew released the bit to fall into the tunnel.

Normally gases in a tunnel are removed from the tunnel through ventilation shafts but there were not any ventilation shafts along the six miles from the water intake and the shore side elevator shaft.

When the heavy steel bit was released and it fell to the bottom of the tunnel, a spark created by the steel striking the concrete ignited the methane gas and triggered a tremendous explosion!

A small portion of the shock wave of the detonation was channeled up the 23-inch bore hole but the majority of the energy shot through the 16-foot diameter horizontal shaft at thousands of miles-per-hour, from the intake towards the elevator shaft.

170

PORT HURON TUNNEL EXPLOSION

The blast shot a jet of dirt and debris up the elevator shaft and 200 hundred feet into the air. Witnesses reported it sounded like a sonic boom from an airplane breaking the sound barrier followed by the exhaust of a jet engine.

The men working in the tunnel were in the path of the blast. Twelve men near the elevator, furthest from the blast epicenter, helped eight other seriously injured men up the elevator shaft to safety. The elevator was not damaged in the explosion.

In the shaft, the corrugated metal air ducts suspended from the roof of the tunnel were ripped to shreds and twisted like tin foil. Pieces of the air duct were blown through the tunnel like sharp deadly shrapnel. A 15-ton crane in the tunnel was blown 57 feet down the shaft and twisted and distorted, a several ton gantry was moved in the blast and anything laying loose was hurled down the shaft as if it was shot out of a rifle.

Damage in the tunnel after the explosion. From the Port Huron Museum.

MONDAY
DECEMBER 13, 1971
PRICE 15 CENTS

THE TIMES HERALD

PORT HURON, MICHIGAN

WEATHER

NOT SO COLD;
SNOW TUESDAY

(Details on
Page 6A)

Serving The Entire Thumb And River Districts   Member Of The Gannett Group

Toll At 22 As Probe Begins

Rescuers quickly responded to the explosion and went down the elevator shaft to look for men in need. They descended into darkness since the electric lights, which illuminated the shaft, had been destroyed by the blast. The rescuers: firemen, ambulance personnel, doctors, and experienced tunnel men, were weakened by the carnage and destruction they found in the tunnel.

The men caught in the blast had been viscously torn apart by the shock wave and the projectiles shot through the tunnel. The shock wave ripped clothing off the men; their bodies were strewn about, some with limbs ripped off by the explosion. Some were decapitated.

Some men were not killed instantly in the explosion, but were trapped in the tangle of debris that extended for a distance of 1,000 feet down the tunnel. Medical personnel tried to make them comfortable as a construction crew cleared away the snarl of metal blocking the tunnel.

From the time of the blast, crews of men worked at looking for anyone in the shaft that might still be alive and removing them to the surface for medical treatment. At 8:00 pm the rescuers were called from the tunnel when methane levels grew dangerously high and fear of another explosion and the loss of more men was a serious threat. Everyone was called from the shaft until fans were set up to ventilate the methane to a tolerable level.

As the dead tunnel men in yellow plastic bags came up the elevator shaft and were placed in waiting ambulances, accusations of negligence and lax safety standards were made and questions were being asked about the explosion. Why didn't the gas monitoring equipment installed in the shaft warn the men of the impending danger? Why did the cofferdam crew drill into the shaft while the shore side crew was in the shaft? Why wasn't the shaft ventilated from the intake end for a distance of five miles?

An 18-member committee was established to determine the cause of the terrible accident that took the lives of 22 men working 230 feet below the surface on the Detroit Metropolitan Water System project.

All agreed that the gas was the result of methane gas leaking into the shaft from pockets in the Antrim shale. The source of ignition is open to

172

PORT HURON TUNNEL EXPLOSION

debate. Some adamantly argue the 23-inch boring bit used at the intake end of the shaft created a spark, yet others suggest smoking construction workers or propane torches used in the shaft were responsible for the explosion.

A memorial to the twenty-two men killed in the explosion in the water intake tunnel was erected near the water treatment plant on Metcalf road north of Port Huron, Michigan.

Below are the names of the men who lost their lives in the explosion in the Port Huron water tunnel project:

Manuel Abasta, 31	Romualdo Alvares, 40
James Beesely, 34	Vernard Woolstenhulme, 63
Roswell Brown, 43	Raymond N. Comeau, 35
Gerald Curtis, 32	Walter J. Woods, 36
Patrick Dingman, 35	Charles Epperson, 44
Donald Fogal Jr., 21	Donald Williams, 44
Donald Hardel, 30	Kenneth Hawes, 33
Martin Laretz, 25	Keith Verner, 21
Frank E. Polk, 27	James Reighard, 30
Gary Roehm, 20	Glen Verner, 44
Claybourne Simkins, 38	Guillermo Teran, 36

THE IROQUOIS
THEATER FIRE

November 20, 1903, marked the long awaited grand opening of Chicago's Iroquois Theater. It had been touted as the most opulent and modern theater in the world.

It's developers selected a location near Chicago's famed Loop, at 24-28 West Randolph between State and Dearborn streets.

They hired renowned theatrical architect Benjamin Marshall and told him they wanted a theater without equal. When finished in November, 1903, Chicago was home to one of the greatest theaters in the world.

The front of the building was polished granite and glazed terra cotta. Twelve ornate doors lead to the foyer that was finished in white Vermont marble inlaid with mosaic. A grand stairway dominated the foyer leading up to the second and third levels. On the dome ceiling was a beautiful mosaic depicting the history of theater in Chicago.

The Grand Stairway of the Iroquois Theater.

On the first level or orchestra level was the most expensive seating. There were very few seats and each was strategically placed so one seat was not directly behind another providing each theatergoer an unobstructed view of the performance and the utmost comfort.

Behind the stage was where most innovation was found. The stage area was fifty feet deep and equipped with only the best and newest of theatrical apparatuses.

There were eighty dressing rooms with walls of enameled brick. The dressing rooms were arranged behind the stage on five floors complete with an elevator to transport the actors to the stage. There was also a dining area, a wardrobe room, a sewing room, a music practice room and a ballet room. And the fly gallery, where the scenery was hung above the stage, was unusually large for theaters of the day.

The beautiful entryway of the Iroquois Theater.

No money was spared to make the Iroquois one of the best, if not the best theater in the world. It was even promoted as being a fireproof playhouse. But as would be seen, money was spared on safety concerns.

On December 30, 1903, a little over a month after its grand opening, the theater was featuring a performance of Klaw & Erlanger's Drury Lane spectacle, "Mr. Bluebeard" starring comedian Eddy Foy.

The Wednesday matinee was sold out, there was standing room only. It is estimated that nearly 1,900 people attended the matinee that day. Schools were out for Christmas vacation and the audience was mostly school age children and their mothers. Near the close of the second act, tragedy struck.

At 3:15, as the actors were singing *"The Pale Moonlight,"* a crewman was shining an arc light on the stage for the pale moon effect. The arc light threw out a spark. The spark struck a small drapery hanging along a wall to the right of the stage. The light operator tried to pat out the fire but could not reach it as the flame raced up the drape. The fire quickly advanced up the sash into the fly gallery, out of sight of the audience.

In the fly gallery, thousands of square feet of canvas scenery covered with flammable paint ignited. Flames quickly jumped from one painted canvas to another, the actors below oblivious of the horror growing above them.

Suddenly flaming fragments of canvas began to rain down on the stage. The orchestra continued to play as the actors quit singing and dancing and began to run from the stage, some with costumes set ablaze from the shower.

The audience slowly realized what was happening. Some rose to run but Eddy Foy, the much-loved star of the play, ran onto the stage and pleaded.

"Ladies and gentlemen, there is no danger. Don't get excited. Walk out calmly."

The curtain was made with asbestos to protect the audience from a stage fire. The stagehands began to lower the curtain, however the curtain could not be fully lowered. It stuck about halfway down.

It was later found a wire running from the back stage out above the audience where an actor would hang as part of the play prevented the curtain from lowering.

As the scenery hanging in the gallery burst into flames and burned with intense heat, the fire could not be isolated from the audience. The heat and

Chicago Tribune *drawing depicting the locked exit doors of the Iroquois Theater.*

flames shot out from the stage, instantly incinerating those sitting in the first few rows of the three levels and igniting anything flammable. Others seated in the auditorium died a suffering death as they inhaled the heated air, falling dead at first breath. The auditorium went dark as the electrical lines were burned.

Thick black smoke quickly filled the auditorium. People tripped and fell over seats and bodies in their mad attempt to escape certain death.

The audience on upper levels began running towards the grand stairway and the exits of the theater. Men, women and children all attempted to descend the Grand Stairway from the second and third levels.

The audience descending the grand stairway shoved and pushed in a panic, knocking children and others down. The crowd stepped over the fallen, trampled them, or tripped over them and fell and were trampled to death.

People fell to their death as they were pushed over the railing by the stampeding audience. The body of a 12-year-old girl was found impaled on a decorative spire of the stairway after apparently falling or being pushed from the third balcony.

The panicked mass racing from the fire was met with locked exit doors, locked by management to prevent people from sneaking in without buying a ticket. Some exit doors were not marked in any way and others were covered with decorative drapery and could not be found in the dark smoke filled auditorium.

The first few who reached the locked doors were crushed against the doors by the flood of people behind them. Their bodies fell at the base of the door and others suffering from smoke inhalation and burns clawed and climbed at the dead and dying trying to escape through the locked doors. Clothing was ripped, eyes were gouged, and hair was pulled by the panicking mass.

THE IROQUOIS THEATER FIRE

As more people attempted to escape from the locked doors, they climbed the human pile, those on the bottom were crushed to death. The victims were found on top of each other stacked as high as seven feet.

Women and children on the third balcony ran to the emergency exits, opened the doors to find the fire escapes had not yet been installed. The people standing at the open door staring down at the concrete three stories below were pushed to their death by others coming behind them trying to flee.

Families became separated, husbands from wives, children from parents. An infant was found on the stairway, trampled to death, when it apparently became separated from its mother's loving grasp.

A screaming woman hysterically ran up to two men, Bill Corbett and Charlie Dexter, outside the theater. She pleaded with the men to help her find her children who were still in the burning theater. The two men, without a thought to their own safety, ran into the building.

The interior of the Iroquois Theater after the devastating fire.

The orchestra level after the fire.

They entered a side hall trying to get to the auditorium. The men groped their way in the narrow, dark and smoke filled room until they came to a door. It took the strength of both men to pull the door open and they were met with a grizzly scene; dead and dying piled one on top of another, mostly women and children, burned and bloodied, stacked like cordwood as they attempted to escape the smoke and fire. Moans and feeble cries came from the pile.

Determined to rescue those still alive, Bill and Charlie began to untangle the mass. They grabbed the arm of a young girl to pull her body from the heap and the burnt flesh simply stripped off her arm. Some of the victims in the heap were unrecognizable; their faces had been trampled and crushed.

Children and women made up the majority of the stack of humanity. Their small hands burned, their clothing ripped, their cold dead eyes staring in horror.

The men had to overcome their shock and disbelief to try to save those still alive. They pulled at the bodies trying to untangle the knotted and

THE IROQUOIS THEATER FIRE

twisted mass of humanity. The dead were cast aside and those alive were carried out of the building.

Peter Quinn, a railroad special inspector, happened to be walking by the theater when he saw a man run from the building. The man ran up to a policeman, told him something and the officer ran off. Mr. Quinn followed the man to the alley where he heard a commotion at a stage door. The door was opened just a few inches. When he looked inside he realized the situation. Actors and stagehands were attempting to flee the burning stage but the mass of humanity was pressing against the door so tightly the escaping crowd could not pull the door open. Mr. Quinn yelled through the crack of the door, pleading with the people to back up so the door could be opened, but there was no response. The crowd didn't move, they were packed so tightly they couldn't move. Fortunately Mr. Quinn was carrying some small tools. He was able to remove the pins from the hinges, the door was cast aside, and the people trapped on stage were able to rush out to safety. If it had not been for Mr. Quinn, those hundred plus would have been added to the death toll.

While firemen fought the fire, police officers and citizens began the gruesome task of removing the dead and dying from the building, a job that lasted well into the following day. The dead were placed on any available carriage and wagon and taken to morgues throughout the city. The victims still alive were rushed to area hospitals.

Bodies of the dead filled all of the Chicago area morgues. From the time bodies first arrived, there was a stream of husbands looking for wives, wives looking for husbands and parents looking for children.

Some bodies did not look as though they had been through a fire, they were not burned, their clothing not singed or charred. These unfortunate souls died from breathing in toxic gases, a by-product of the fire. Other bodies were unrecognizable for they had been trampled, their heads crushed, their faces smashed, their bodies broken under the weight of those fleeing the fire. On the extreme were the bodies of women, men and children that had been burnt so badly that all that remained were shriveled blackened fragments of what was just a few hours ago a healthy viable person.

After the identification of the dead was completed, after the funerals, after the tears slowed, a coroner's inquest was begun. The theater owners, the theater's fire marshal, the city fire inspectors, and many other theater employees were indicted and brought up on charges for their actions that resulted in six hundred plus deaths.

There were many building code violations that attributed to the death toll. There was no sprinkler system, yet the Chicago building code specifically dictated it must have a system. There were too few exit doors and too many exit doors were locked. There were exit doors covered with decorative drapery making it impossible to find them in a smoke filled room. Not all exits were marked with signs and none of the signs were lit. There were decorative iron gates at the third level designed to keep people from moving down to better seats during the performance and the third floor fire escapes were not installed.

A wagon used to carry the unfortunate souls that lost their life in the fire to the morgue.

After four years of legal wrangling, many of the men brought up on charges were found guilty but none received any punishment.

On December 30, 1903, nearly 1,900 people entered the Iroquois Theater to watch the beloved American comedian Eddy Foy in the play "Mr. Bluebeard". Unfortunately, not all of them left alive.

In the mad rush to leave the raging inferno, an estimated 575 men women and children died, hundreds more were injured and there were at least thirty additional deaths as a result of the injuries. The Chicago Iroquois Theater Fire is the deadliest single building fire in the history of the United States.

> *"The screams of the children for their mothers and mothers for their children I shall carry in my memory to my dying day."* — Frank Slosson, survivor.

CAL POLY
FIGHTING MUSTANGS

The Bowling Green Falcons and the Mustangs of the California Polytechnic College were set to meet on the football field Saturday, October 29, 1960.

The Mustang's season was not going as well as they had hoped; they had just one win and four losses on the season. The team had hoped to do as well as they had two years earlier when All Conference Offense Tackle John Madden, was an outstanding offensive and defensive player for the Mustangs.

The Bowling Green Falcons, on the other hand, were ranked the second best small college in the nation. When they took to the field to battle the Mustangs they would be defending an undefeated season.

The game was being played in Bowling Green so the Mustangs would leave California on October 27, fly to Toledo and take a bus to Bowling Green, Ohio, and stay in a motel until the game.

The two teams took to the field on October 29th but the game did not go well for the Cal Poly Mustangs. The Mustang quarterback, Ted Toller (who went on to a stellar college and NFL coaching career) came out throwing the ball, completing 18 of 32 passes for 246 yards, but the Cal Poly defense could not stop the Bowling Green Falcons.

Bowling Green ran and passed at will. The Falcons led by a 14-0 score after the first quarter and took a 27-0 lead into halftime. Cal Poly scored in the third quarter but failed to make the conversion while the Falcons scored on a nine yard run. The fourth quarter was all Bowling green as they scored 16 unanswered points making the final score 50-6.

All the Mustangs had to look forward to was another bus ride and a long airplane ride back to northern California, where they would lick their wounds and prepare for their next game.

The team's Arctic – Pacific Airlines charter airplane was at the Toledo, Ohio, Express Airport preparing to transport the team back to California, but it had not been just sitting idle waiting for them, the propeller airplane had been busy.

Bowling Green Breezes Past California Poly Tech, 50-6

The aircraft the Mustangs were using was a Curtis Wright Super C-46 F propeller airplane chartered by Arctic – Pacific Airlines. The C-46, a World War II vintage transport plane, was commonly used in small charter companies for cargo hauling and in the passenger market.

The Arctic – Pacific C-46, tail number N 1244N, that was transporting the team originated its flight on October 27th at its home base in Oakland, California. From there the flight crew, Captain Donald Chesher and Co-Pilot Howard Perovich and an in flight hostess flew to Santa Maria, California, to pick up the Cal Poly football team. With 48 passengers and crew aboard, the twin engine propeller plane flew to Albuquerque, New Mexico, to take on fuel.

The next stop for the Arctic – Pacific flight was at Kansas City, Missouri where a pilot and co-pilot that were catching a ride disembarked. The aircraft then flew to Toledo, Ohio, with 46 onboard. In Toledo, the Cal Poly Football team disembarked and the flight crew took off for Youngstown, Ohio.

The flight crew laid over in Youngstown and in the morning boarded the Youngstown University football team for a non-stop flight to their game in New Haven, Connecticut.

After a 30 hour layover in Connecticut, the airplane flew the Youngstown University football team from New Haven back to Youngstown then they ferried the aircraft back to Toledo where they would board the Cal Poly football team. From Toledo they would fly to Kansas City to pick up flight crew left there, then on to Santa Maria to drop off the football team and back to its home base at Oakland, California.

On the morning of Saturday, October 29, the aircraft with Captain Donald Chesher and Co-Pilot Howard Perovich in the right and left seats and Stewardess Susan Miller flew to Toledo. When they landed in Toledo there was only ¾ mile visibility due to a heavy fog.

Flight N 1244N was refueled, taking on 477 gallons of high octane aviation fuel, making a total of 1,062 gallons onboard. The engines were checked and 2 gallons of oil was added to the right engine and the left engine took seven gallons.

Captain Chesher met with the meteorologist at the airport for an update on conditions. He then walked the ramp through the fog locating where airplanes were parked. He would need to know where the planes were when he taxied to the runway through the fog.

Shortly before 2:00 pm, the aircraft was loaded with 46 passengers and crew and parked at the Remmert-Werner ramp. The visibility had not improved and it was still very limited.

Captain Chesher started the engines and radioed the tower for clearance. He was instructed to use runway 25 and warned of the unlighted aircraft parked on the ramp.

The re-fueling crew guided the aircraft to the taxiway with flashlights. They later said visibility was less than 200 feet.

Arctic – Pacific Airlines had established minimum take off conditions for all airports they fly out of. Their minimums for takeoff at the Toledo Express Airport was 300 foot ceiling and 1 mile visibility or 3/4th of a mile visibility with a 400 foot ceiling. The meteorologist recorded the conditions at the time of take off were zero visibility due to fog and 9/10ths of the sky obscured.

Captain Chesher taxied the aircraft to the threshold of the runway and awaited clearance. The tower asked how many runway lights he could see in front of him. He responded he could see three lights ahead through the fog. Captain Chesher then asked how far apart the lights were. The lights were 200 feet apart.

According to federal regulations the air traffic controller at the Toledo Express Airport tower could not deny take off clearance to an aircraft because of weather conditions; it was a decision left to the pilot. Captain Chesher elected to stay on schedule and take off in spite of the limited visibility.

The fog obscured the view from the tower. Tower personnel could not see the aircraft but heard it power up. The aircraft slowly began to roll down the runway gaining speed. Passengers reported as the aircraft gained ground speed the plane swerved to the right and then sharply to the left just before liftoff.

As the C-46 struggled to climb, a vibration shook the aircraft, people on the ground unable to see the airplane through the fog said they heard a change in the sound of the engines during liftoff and climb. The left wing of the Curtis Wright Super C-46 F dipped and the aircraft went into a slow left bank as the left engine experienced a partial loss of power. The nose of the airplane dipped with the loss of propulsion and the aircraft lost lift.

The left wingtip banked at a 60 to 90 degree angle to the ground and struck the taxiway adjacent to the runway and the C-46 cartwheeled across the ground. Pieces of the aircraft, luggage, cargo and passengers were thrown from the airliner as it flipped end over end.

The C-46 came to rest 400 feet left of the center of the runway, 5,800 feet from roll off. The fuselage containing 43 passengers broke in half. The forward section burst into flames as the 1,062 gallons of high octane aviation fuel spewed from the ruptured tanks. The aft section lay upside down several feet away.

Many passengers were thrown from the cartwheeling airplane and were found strewn about on the taxiway. Passengers were found wandering around in shock three hundred feet from the impact zone. Some passengers were still strapped in their seats as they were ejected from the aircraft. Five surviving passengers remained strapped in their seats in the aft section hanging in the inverted wreckage. There was no fuel in the aft tanks of the C-46 and it did not catch on fire.

Two Mustang football players, Jim Fahey and Don Adams, survived the crash and braved the flames climbing hundreds of feet in the air and the intense heat to pull teammates from the burning forward section.

Airport ground support personnel who heard the crash, and members of the Air National Guard who were having a Halloween party in a nearby hanger, rushed to the wreckage. Ambulance and fire fighting equipment had difficulty getting to the scene because of the thick fog.

Twenty-two people were killed in the crash, 24 survived but suffered injuries ranging from bruises and shock to broken and shattered bones and severe burns.

The lives of 46 people in the accident of Arctic-Pacific Airlines were forever changed on that October day in 1960, not to mention the life shattering changes for the mothers, fathers, wives and children of those killed and injured.

The Civil Aeronautics Board investigated the crash that took the lives of 22 people and found there were several contributing factors which attributed to the devastating accident.

Cal Poly Students Mourn for Grid Team at Special Rites

SAN LUIS OBISPO, Oct. 31

CAL POLY FIGHTING MUSTANGS

Clovis News-Journal

"YOUR FREEDOM NEWSPAPER"

VOL. 42 NO. 196   UPI Leased Wire   NEA, McNaught Features   CLOVIS, NEW MEXICO, SUNDAY, NOVEMBER 15, 1970   42 PAGES TODAY   DAILY OR SUNDAY 10¢

75 Believed Dead In Airplane Crash

Football Team Among Victims

The C-46 was found to be 2,000 pounds over its certified takeoff weight. The excessive weight resulted in the airplane fishtailing or swerving while it rolled down the runway. The pilot, having trouble keeping the aircraft straight on the runway lifted off prematurely to avoid more swerving and possibly loss of control, even though the C-46 had not reached the recommended takeoff speed.

The Civil Aeronautics Board noted both the pilot and co-pilot had been on flight duty for more than 26 hours. This far exceeded the recommended duty duration.

As a result of the tragic accident that resulted in the death of 16 members of the Cal Poly Football team, the Federal Aviation Authority revised its regulations giving the air traffic controllers the authority to deny take off clearance to aircraft during adverse weather conditions.

A memorial has been erected on the campus of the California State Polytechnic College honoring those who died in the accident. The Cal Poly football team disaster was the first airplane crash involving a college or professional athletic team, but it was not the last. Two other schools have erected memorials to athletic teams who were victims of horrid airplane accidents.

Ten years after the Cal Poly accident, on October 2, 1970, one of two jet airliners, a Martin 404, carrying 36 members of the Wichita State University football team fans and coaching staff crashed into a mountain near Silver Plume, Colorado. Thirty one passengers and crew were killed while en route to a football game at Logan, Utah, at Utah State University.

The accident was deemed by Federal Aviation authorities to be the result of pilot error. The pilot took a route through a mountain valley where the aircraft could neither fly over terrain that obstructed his course nor offered enough room to turn around.

GREAT LAKES DISASTERS

Just over a month later on November 14, 1970, Southern Airways Flight 932, a DC-9, crashed while flying from Kinston, North Carolina, to Ceredo, West Virgina. The accident killed all seventy five onboard; 37 members of the Marshall University Thundering Herd football team, 8 members of the coaching staff, 25 team boosters and the fight crew.

While on final approach in rain, fog, smoke and overcast conditions the aircraft had descended below minimal acceptable levels and struck trees on a hill a mile from the runway. The aircraft, not able to maintain flight, crashed to the ground cutting a swath through the forest 95 feet wide and 279 feet long. The DC-9 was totally destroyed and all onboard were killed.

REFERENCES

The Great Fires of 1871

Absolute Michigan, All Michigan, All the time, "The Great Michigan Fire of 1871", http://www.absolutemichigan.com/dig/michigan/the-great-michigan-fire-of-1871/

American Experience; Chicago, City of the Century, http://www.pbs.org/wgbh/amex/chicago/index.html

Chicago Historical Society, "The Great Chicago Fire", http://www.chicagohs.org/history/fire.html

Deana C. Hipke. *The Great Peshtigo Fire of 1871.* http://www.peshtigofire.info/

Everything, "Peshtigo Fire",http://everything2.com/title/Peshtigo+Fire

Firestorms of 1871, www.boisestate.edu/history/ncasner/hy210/peshtigo.htm

Michigan Fire Service.com, "Great Thumb Forest Fire", September 1, 2008, http://michiganfireservice.com/great-thumb-forest-fire/101/

Newspaper articles at *The Wisconsin Reader* site at www.library.wisc.edu

Peshtigo Fire Page, www.rootsweb.com/~wioconto/Fire.htm
Peshtigo: a tornado of fire revisited, news.mpr.org/features/200211/27_hemphills_peshtigofire

Rootsweb, "The Great fire of 1871, History of Manistee County, Michigan", http://www.rootsweb.ancestry.com/~mimanist/ManHist14.html

Tales of Heroism and Tragedy Swirl Around the Fire the *Green Bay Press-Gazette*, http://www.crh.noaa.gov/grb/PeshtigoFire.html

The Great Chicago Fire, Horace White, Editor and chief of the *Chicago Tribune* (in 1871) http://www.nationalcenter.org,Chicagofire.html

The Herald and *Torch Light*, Hagerstown, MD, December 27, 1871.

The Janesville Gazette, Janesville, Wisconsin, October 14, 27, 1871.

The Janesville Gazette, Janesville, Wisconsin, November 1, 1871.

The Great Peshtigo Fire of 1871, www.peshtigofire.info

University of Michigan News Service, Fires ravaged Michigan's thumb in 1871, 1881, MICHIGAN HISTORY SERIES, http://ns.umich.edu/htdocs/releases/story.php?id=1245

United States History, Great Peshtigo Fire, http://www.u-s-history.com/pages/h2113.html

Wisconsin State Journal, Madison, Wisconsin, October 12, 1871.

Wikipedia, the free encyclopedia, "Port Huron Fire of 1871", http://en.wikipedia.org/wiki/Port_Huron_Fire_of_1871

Wikipedia the free encyclopedia, "The Great Chicago Fire", http://en.wikipedia.org/wiki/Great_Chicago_Fire

GREAT LAKES DISASTERS

The Great Storm of 1913

Deedler, William, R., "Hell Hath' No Fury Like a Great Lakes Fall Storm; Great Lakes White Hurricane November 1913." http://www.crh.noaa.gov/dtx/stm_1913.htm

Doner, Mary Francis, "The Salvager, The life of Captain Tom Reid on the Great Lakes." Ross and Haines Inc., Minneapolis, Minnesota, 1958.

Historical Collection of the Great Lakes, Bowling Green State University.

Swayze, David D., *Shipwreck!*, Harbor House Publishers, Inc., Boyne City, Michigan, 1992.

The New York Times, New York, New York, November 13, 1913.

The Daily Review, Decatur, Illinois, November 14, 1913

When Ships Collide; the Story of the *Lady Elgin*

Grand Traverse Herald Weekly, September 14, 1860

http://www.lakemagazine.com/poetry/ladyelgin.html

Historical Collection of the Great Lakes, Bowling Green State University

History of the Great Lakes, http://www.mfhn.com/glsdb/archivestemp/ldyelgin.html

Marine disaster, http://www.linkstothepast.com

The Wreck of the Lady Elgin, Brendon Baillod, http://www.baillod.com/elgin//milwaukee/marinrdis.html

Swayze, David D., *Shipwreck!*, Harbor House Publishers, Inc., Boyne City, Michigan, 1992

Wreck of the Steamer Lady Elgin, Brendon Baillod, http://my.expecpc.com/~drewitz/elginh

The Madman of Bath, Michigan

Bath School Disaster, Wikipedia, http://www.wikipedia.org.

Bath Massacre, Arnie, Bernstein, University of Michigan Press, 2009.

essortment, "The bombing of the Bath Consolidated Schools" http://www.essort-ment.com

Rootsweb, "The Bath School Disaster" http://www.freepages.history,rootswebancestry.com

The Bath School Disaster, Monty J. Ellsworth, 1927.

The Mediadrome, "Just another Sunny Day: The Bath School Disaster" http://www.themediadrome.com

The State Journal, Lansing, Michigan, May 18, 1927

TruTv Crime Library, Mark Gado, "Hell Comes to Bath", http://www.trytv.com

The News-Palladium, Benton Harbor, Michigan, August 11, 1966.

The Lima News, Lima, Ohio, May 19, 1927.

The Ludington Daily News, Ludington, Michigan, May 18, 1927.

REFERENCES

Cleveland Explosion of 1944

AP News Wire Releases, October 21, 1944 and October 23, 1944.

All Things Cleveland, Ohio, The Cleveland East Ohio Gas Explosion of 1944, http://allthingsclevelandohio.blogspot.com/2008/12/cleveland-east-ohio-gas-explosion-of.html

New Castle News - October 21, 1944, New Castle, Pennsylvania

The Chicago Tribune, Chicago, Illinois, October 22, 1944.

The Detroit Free Press, Detroit, Michigan, October 21, 22, 1944.

The Sunday Times Signal, Zaneville, Ohio, October 21, 1944.

Wikipedia, the free encyclopedia, Cleveland East Ohio Gas Explosion, http://en.wikipedia.org/wiki/Cleveland_East_Ohio_Gas_explosion

The Cherry Mine Disaster

Buck, Frank, "The Cherry Coal Mine Disaster", 1910.

Cherry Coal Mine Disaster, Ray Tutaj, Jr., http://guitarjourney.tripod.com/-cherrycoalminedisaster/

Illinois Labor History Society, "Story of the Great Cherry Coal Mine Disaster", http://www.kentlaw.edu/ilhs/cherrymi.htm

Pantagraph.com, 100 years later, tragedy of Cherry Mine disaster still hits home, http://www.pantagraph.com/news/article_837d60e3-7dd8-556c-b595-0a7fdaac7b5b.html

The Chicago Daily Tribune, Chicago, Illinois, November 15, 16, 1909.

The New York Times, New York, New York, November 28, 1909.

The State of Illinois Bureau of Labor Statistics, "The Cherry Mine Disaster", Library of the University of Illinois Urbana-Champaign, Springfield, Illinois, 1910.

United States Mine Rescue Association, Historical Data on Mine Disasters in the United States, "Story of the Great Cherry Coal Mine Disaster", http://www.usmra.com/saxsewell/historical.htm

S.S. Eastland: The Worst Disaster on the Great Lakes

Bell System Memorial, http://www.bellsysyemmemorial.com/eastland.html

Chicago Historical Information, http://www.chipublic.org/004chicago'disasters/eastland_photos.html

Eastland Disaster Historical Society, http://eastlanddisaster.org.html

Hilton, George, W., "*Eastland* Legacy of the *Titanic*", Stanford University Press, Stanford, California, 1995

Historical Collection of the Great Lakes, Bowling Green State University

Swayze, David D., *Shipwreck!*, Harbor House Publishers, Inc., Boyne City, Michigan, 1992

GREAT LAKES DISASTERS

The Chicago Sunday Tribune, July 25, 1915

The Daily News, Lake Steamer capsizes in Chicago River, http://www.inficad.com/~ksup/pm_oct15.html

The *Eastland*, http://www.rmstitanichistory.com/eastland.html

The *Eastland* Disaster, http://chicago.about.com/library/blank/bleastland01.html

The *Eastland* Disaster of 1915, http://www.novagate.net/~bonevelle/eastland/

The Huron County Independent, July 30, 1915.

Centralia Coal Mine Disaster

Chicago Daily Tribune, Chicago, Illinois, March 26, 27, 1947.

CHS Class of 68, Centralia No. 5 Mine Disaster, http://www.chs68.com/minedisaster/

Edwardsville Intelligencer, Edwardsville, Illinois, March 26, 1947.

Fanning, Fred, "Public Sector Safety Professionals: Focused on Activity or Results?" http://www.asse.org/practicespecialties/publicsector/docs/PSPS%20Best-of-the-Best%20Newsletter%20Article%202006-2007.pdf

Gendisaster, *Events that Touched our Ancestors Lives, Centralia Coal Mine Disaster, March 1947.*

http://www3.gendisasters.com/illinois/5822/centralia-il-coal-mine-disaster-mar-1947

The Illinois Labor History Society, The Centralia Mine Disaster, http://www.kentlaw.edu/ilhs/centrali.htm

United States Mine Rescue Association, Historical Data on Mine Disasters in the United States, http://www.usmra.com/saxsewell/historical.htm

Hammond Circus Train Disasters

Freeport Journal-Standard, Freeport, Indiana, June 22, 1918.

GenDisasters, *Events that touched our Ancestors Lives*, Hammond, Indiana, Hagenbeck-Wallace Circus Train Wreck, June 18, 1918, http://www.gendisasters.com/data1/in/trains/hammond-circustrainwreck1918.htm

Hagenbeck – Wallace Circus in the United States, http://www.elephant.se/location2.php?location_id=574

Hammondindiana.com, "Online City Guide", Hammond, Indiana, *Hagenbeck-Wallace Circus Train Wreck,* June 18, 1918, http://www.hammondindiana.com/history/circus.htm

Potterville Review, Potterville, Iowa, June 22, 1918.

The Chicago Tribune, Chicago, Illinois, June 23, 24, 1918.

The Lowel Sun, August 8, 1903.

The Newark Advocate, Newark, Ohio, August 7, 1903.

The New York Times, New York, New York, June 23, 1918.

REFERENCES

Timelines, What Happened on June 18, 1918, http://timelines.com/what-happened-on/6/22

The Crash of United Airlines Boeing 247

AvStop.com, An Aviation Online Magazine, "History of United Airlines", http://avstop.com/history/historyofairlines/united_airlines.htm

Chicago Daily Tribune, Chicago, Illinois, October 11, 1933.

Enotes.com, "United Airlines Chesterton Crash," http://www.enotes.com/topic/United_Airlines_Chesterton_Crash

Nevada State journal, Reno, Nevada, October 11, 1933.

The Star Journal, Sandusky, Ohio, October 11, 1933.

Wikipedia, the free encyclopedia, The United Airlines Chesterton Crash, http://en.wikipedia.org/wiki/United_Airlines_Chesterton_Crash

The Sinking of the *Edmund Fitzgerald*

Department of Transportation Coast Guard Marine Casualty Report. *SS Edmund Fitzgerald*; sinking in Lake Superior on November 10, 1975 with loss of life. U.S. Coast Guard Marine Board of Investigation report and Commandant's Action, Report No. USCG 16732/64216

Detroit Free Press, Detroit, Michigan, November 11, 12, 1975.

Detroit News, Detroit, Michigan, November 11, 12, 13, 1975

National Transportation Safety Board, Washington, D.C. 20594, Marine Accident Report *SS Edmund Fitzgerald* sinking in Lake Superior, November 10, 1975, Report Number: NTSB-Mar-78-3.

"Significant Events in the History of the *Edmund Fitzgerald*", Compiled by Tony Wesley. http://tonywesley.com/edm-fritz.html

Stonehouse, Frederick, "The Wreck of the *Edmund Fitzgerald*," Avery Color Studios, Inc., Gwinn, Michigan, 2006.

Swayze, David D., "Shipwreck! A Comprehenshive Directory of over 3,700 Shipwrecks on the Great Lakes." Harbor House Publishing, Boyne City, Michigan, 1992.

Telescope, 40th Anniversary Launch of the *S.S. Edmund Fitzgerald*; $8 Million Dollar~7500 Ton Laker is Born, May- August, 1998, Volume XLVI; Number 2

The Evening News, Sault Ste. Marie, Michigan, November 11, 12, 13,14,15, 1975.

The Sinking of the *SS Edmund Fitzgerald* – November 10, 1975, http://cimss.ssec.wisc.edu/wxwise/fitz.html

Flight 191 – Chicago to Los Angeles

Airdisasters.com, Solutions for safer skies, Special Report, American Airlines Flight 191, Kilroy, Chris, http://www.airdisaster.com/special/specialaa191.shtml

Wikipedia, The free encyclopedia, American Airlines Flight 191, http://en.wikipedia.org/wiki/American_Airlines_Flight_191

www.Aviationexplorer.com, McDonnell Douglas, DC-10, http://www.aviation-explorer.com/dc-10_facts.htm.

Mark Suppelas's Closer Look, Remembering the Crash of Flight 191, http://marksuppelsa.typepad.com/closerlook/2004/05/remembering_the.html

National Transportation Safety Board Aircraft Accident Report, American Airlines DC-10-10 ,N110AA.

Special Report - American Airlines Flight 191, http://191airline.blogspot.com/

TOPIX: Local news of Elk Grove Village, The crash of Flight 191, http://www.topix.com/forum/city/elk-grove-village-il/TFHA38PFQH2JOQHUI

The Metropolitan Store Explosion

Canada.Com, Gallery: Metropolitan Store Explosion, www.windsorstar.com

Canadian Voices, Metropolitan Store Explosion, Community.Canada.com

GenDisasters, Windsor, Ontario Department Store Explosion, Oct 1960, Posted by Stu Beitler. www.gendisaters.com/explosion

The Detroit Free Press, Detroit, Michigan, October 26, 27, 1960.

The Detroit News, Detroit, Michigan, October 26, 1960.

Windsor Fire and Rescue Services, 1960 Explosion Remembered, www.windsorfire.com

Five Days in Hell

"1995 Chicago Heat Wave", Wikipedia, the Free Encyclopedia, http://en.wikipedia.org/wiki/1995_Chicago_heat_wave

Chicago Tribune, Chicago, Illinois, July 14, 15, 16, 17, 18, 19, 20, 1995.

Encyclopedia of Chicago, "Heat Wave of 1995" http://www.encyclopedia.chicagohistory.org/pages/2433.html

NOAA 96-21, Many of the 1995 heat wave deaths were preventable according to NOAA report http://www.publicaffairs.noaa.gov/pr96/apr96/noaa96-21.html

"The 1995 Heat Wave in Chicago Illinois", Jim Angel, state climatologist, Illinois State Water Survey, University of Illinois.

Willis Haviland Carrier, "Father of Cool", The History of Air Conditioning, http://inventors.about.com/library/weekly/aa081797.htm

The Great 1913 Ohio Flood

Severe Weather in Ohio, "March 23-27, 1913: Statewide Flood", http://www.ohiohistory.org

Ohio History Central, an Online Encyclopedia of Ohio History, 1913 Ohio Statewide Flood. http//www.ohiohistorycentral.org

The Chicago Daily Tribune, Chicago, Illinois, March 24, 25, 26, 1913.

The Detroit Free Press, Detroit, Michigan, March 27, 1913.

Tribstar.com; the online version of the Tribune-Star, Terre Haute, Indiana, June

REFERENCES

12, 2008, http//:cber.iweb.bsu.edu/news2008/061208_tribstar.

Wikipedia, the free Encylopedia, Oh Dayton Flood, 1913, http://
en.Wikipedia.org/wiki/file:OH pdfdayton-flood1913-4thst.jpg.

The 1925 Three State Tornado

The Tornado of 1925, Jackson County, Illinois, http://www.carolyar.com/-
Illinois/Misc/Jackson.htm

Popular Mechanics, "Tri-State Tornado: Missouri, Illinois, Indiana, March
1925," http://www.popularmechanics.com/science/environment/natural-
disasters/4219866

NOAA Weather Service, 1925 Tri-State Tornado: A look Back,
http://www.crh.noaa.gov/pah/?n=1925tor

MICHAEL PEARSON ASSOCIATED PRESS, 1925 Monster Tornado killed
hundreds lead to development of warning system., http://smokeys-trail.com/-
tornado/1925.html

Midwest Express Flight 105

Chicago Tribune, Chicago, Illinois, September 6, 1985.

GenDisasters, Events that changed our Ancestors Lives, Milwaukee, WI Jetliner
Crashes On Takeoff Killing 31, Sep 1985, http://www3.gendisasters.com/-
wisconsin/5258/milwaukee,-wi-jetliner-crashes-takeoff-killing-31,-sep-1985.

National Transportation Safety Board, Aircraft Accident Report, Midwest
Airlines Express, Inc., NTSB/AAR-87/01.

Wikipedia, The free encyclopedia, Midwest Express Airlines Flight 105.

Ohio Penitentiary Fire

Delphos Daily Hearld, Delphos, Ohio, May 19, 1931.

Hamilton Daily Journal, Hamilton, Ohio, April 21, 1950.

History.com, This day in history, http://www.history.com/this-day-in-
history/prisoners-left-to-burn-in-ohio-fire

Lowell Sun, Lowell, Massachusetts, April 22, 1930.

Ohio History Central: AN Online Encyclopedia of Ohio History,
http://www.ohiohistorycentral.org/image.php?rec=558&img=969

Timelines, Ohio Prison Fire, http://timelines.com/1930/4/21/ohio-penitentiary-fire

North Lake Mine Disaster

The Daily Northwestern, Oshkosh, Wisconsin, November 5, 1926.

The Detroit News, Detroit, Michigan, November 6, 1926.

Department of Natural Recourses and Environment, Michigan Iron Industry
Museum, http://www.michigan.gov/dnr/0,1607,7-153-54463_18595_18611—-
,00.html

GREAT LAKES DISASTERS

Ironwood Daily Globe, Ironwood, Michigan, November 4, 1926.

Mine Accidents and Disasters: Cleveland Cliffs Iron Company Barnes-Hecker Mine Inundation.

http://www.usmra.com/saxsewell/barnes_hecker.htm

The Manitowoc Herald-News, Manitowoc, Wisconsin, November 4, 1926.

Wisconsin Rapids Daily Tribune, Wisconsin Rapids, Wisconsin, November 4, 1926.

The Our Lady of the Angels School Fire

Alton Evening Telegraph, Alton, Illinois, December 2, 1958.

Chicago Now, "Fire at Our Lady of the Angels (12-1-1958)" http://www.chicagonow.com/blogs/unknown-chicago/2010/12/fire-at-a-chicago-school-12-1-1958.html

Encyclopedia of Chicago, Our Lady of the Angels Fire, http://www.encyclopedia.chicagohistory.org/pages/939.html

Freeport Journal-Standard, Freeport, Illinois, December 2, 1958.

Mount Vernon Register News, Mount Vernon, Illinois, December 2, 1958.

Our Lady of the Angels, A website dedicated to the memory of those who lost their lives and to all those who survived the tragedy. http://www.olafire.com/

Our Lady of the Angels school fire, December 1, 1958, http://archives.archchicago.org/OLAfire.htm

Withthecommand.com, "Our Lady of the Angels: A historical perspective on school fires",
By Thomas M. Cunningham, http://www.withthecommand.com/09-Sept/MD-Ourlady-0904.html

Port Huron Tunnel Explosion

Michigan Safety News, Michigan Safety History – Port Huron Tunnel Explosion, June 28, 2009

http://michigansafetynews.com/michigan-safety-history-port-huron-tunnel-explosion/154

The Detroit News, Detroit, Michigan, "Horror in a Port Huron water intake tunnel", By Vivian M. Baulch /*The Detroit News*, http://apps.detnews.com/apps/history/index.php?id=211#ixzz187fvoSNUhttp://apps.detnews.com/apps/history/index.php?id=211

The Detroit Water and Sewerage Department, Remembering Those Who Died, http://www.dwsd.org/history/explosion.pdf

The News-Palladium, Benton Harbor, Michigan, December 13, 1971.

The Times Herald, Port Huron, Michigan, December 12, 13,14,15,16,17, 1971.

The Traverse City Record Eagle, Traverse City, Michigan, February 10, 1975.

REFERENCES

The Iroquois Theater Fire

"Chicago Death Trap, The Iroquois Theater Fire of 1903," Southern Illinois University Press, 2003.

Chicago Tribune, December 30, 1903, "The Iroquois Theater fire; A fire during a holiday matinee kills hundreds and leads to tougher safety standards nationwide". http://www.chicagotribune.com/news/politics/chi-chicagodays-iroquoisfire-story,0,6395565.story

Decatur Herald, Decatur, Illinois, January 5, 1904.

"LEST WE FORGET", Chicago's Awful Theater Horror, By the survivors and rescuers, The Library of Illinois University, Memorial Publishing, Co., 1904.

Illinois State Archives, "Cook County Coroner's Inquest Record , Iroquois Theater Fire"
http://www.cyberdriveillinois.com/departments/archives/iroqfire.html

Oshkosh Daily Northeasterner, Oshkosh, Wisconsin, November 19, 1903.

The Daily Review, Decatur, Illinois, December 31, 1903.

"The Iroquois Theater Fire," *Cedar Rapids Republican*, Cedar Rapids, Iowa, November 20, 1903

The Racine Daily Journal, Racine, Wisconsin, December 31, 1903.

Cal Poly Fighting Mustangs

Aircraft accident report, Southern Airways, INC. DC-9, N97S, SA-422, File No. 1-0023, Tri-State Airport, Huntington, West Virginia, November 14, 1970.

Arm chair GM, John Madden,
http://armchairgm.wikia.com/John_Madden_(football)

Civil Aeronautics Board Aircraft Accident Report, SA 360. File number 1-0047, Arctic- Pacific Airlines, Inc., Curtis Wright Super C-46 F, N 1244N, Toledo, Ohio, Express Airport, October 29, 1960.

National Transportation Safety Board, Washington, D. C. 20591, sa-421 file no. 3-1127, Aircraft Accident Report, Martin 404, n464m, 8 statute miles west of SilverP, Colorado, October 2,1970

The Coshocton Tribune, Coshocton, Ohio, October 31, 1960.

The Lima News, Lima, Ohio, October 30, 1960.

Toledo Blade, Toledo, Ohio, October 29, 2010

Unofficial Marshall University 1970 Crash, Rocco S. Rossetti, http://users.-marshall.edu/~rossett1/pages/1970/crash.html

ACKNOWLEDGEMENTS

No historical endeavor can be accomplished without the assistance and aid of many. I want to thank all of those who contributed.

Aaron O'Donovan, MLIS, Curator of Digital Collections, Ohio Historical Society.

Bowling Green State University, Historical Collections of the Great Lakes, Bowling Green State University. Robert Graham, Archivist.

Bad Axe Public Library, Bad Axe, Michigan.

Barrow, William C., MA, MLS, Special Collections Librarian Michael Schwartz Library, Cleveland State University.

Bayliss Public Library, Sault St. Marie, Michigan.

Benton Harbor Public Library, Benton Harbor, Michigan.

Crissy Castillo, Director, Durand Union Station, Inc. Durand, Michigan.

City of Harbor Beach, Michigan.

Dossin Great Lakes Museum, John Polacsek, Curator of Marine History, Detroit, Michigan.

Eastland Disaster Society, Ted Wachholz, President and Director, Chicago, Illinois.

Eric Morgan, Webmaster@ola,com, Our Lady of the Angels school.

Freighter Frank in Port Huron, Michigan. www.boatnerd.com.

Harbor Beach Public Library, Harbor Beach, Michigan, Vicki Mazure, Director.

Hugh Clark for his assistance and access to his Great Lakes Photographic Collection.

Library of Michigan, Lansing, Michigan.

Michigan Maritime Museum, South Haven, Michigan.

Point aux Barques Lighthouse Society, Port Hope, Michigan.

Port Huron Museum, Port Huron Michigan.

St. Clair Public Library, Port Huron, Michigan.

United States Coast Guard, Historian's Office.

ABOUT THE AUTHOR

Geography has played an important part in shaping Wayne "Skip" Kadar's love of the Great Lakes. Throughout his life he has lived in the downriver area of Detroit, Marquette, Harbor Beach and at the family cottage in Manistique, Michigan. Growing and living in these rich historic maritime areas has instilled in him a love of the Great Lakes and their maritime past.

Photo by Karen Kadar

This love has taken him in many directions. He is a certified S.C.U.B.A. diver and avid boater, having owned most all types of boats from Personal Water Craft to sailboats to a small cruiser. He is involved in lighthouse restoration, serving as the Vice President of the Harbor Beach Lighthouse Preservation Society.

Mr. Kadar enjoys studying and researching Great Lakes maritime history and has made presentations on maritime history on a local, state and national level.

An educator for thirty years, Mr. Kadar retired after 15 years as a high school principal.

Skip lives in Harbor Beach, Michigan, with his wife Karen. During the summer, Skip can usually be found at the Harbor Beach Marina, on the family boat "Pirate's Lady" or at the lighthouse.

**Other Wayne Kadar Titles by
Avery Color Studios:**

*Great Lakes Cold Case Files
Unsolved Murders of the Great Lakes Region*

*Great Lakes Serial Killers,
True Accounts of the Great Lakes Most Gruesome Murders*

Strange & Unusual Shipwrecks On The Great Lakes

Avery Color Studios, Inc. has a full line of Great Lakes oriented books, puzzles, cookbooks, shipwreck and lighthouse maps, posters, stickers and magnets.

For a full color catalog call:
1-800-722-9925

Avery Color Studios, Inc. products are available at gift shops and bookstores throughout the Great Lakes region.